One Step at a Time, Intermediate 1

Judith D. García

Miami-Dade Community College
Kendall Campus

I(T)P

Heinle & Heinle Publishers
An International Thomson Publishing Company
Boston, Massachusetts, 02116, USA

Heinle & Heinle Publishers
20 Park Plaza
Boston, MA 02116 U.S.A.

International Thomson Publishing
Berkshire House 168–173
High Holborn
London WC1V7AA
England

Thomas Nelson Australia
102 Dodds Street
South Melbourne, 3205
Victoria, Australia

Nelson Canada
1120 Birchmont Road
Scarborough, Ontario
Canada M1K5G4

International Thomson
  Publishing Gmbh
Königwinterer Strasse 418
53227 Bonn
Germany

International Thomson
  Publishing Asia
Block 221 Henderson Road
#08–03
Henderson Industrial Park
Singapore 0315

International Thomson
  Publishing—Japan
Hirakawacho-cho Kyowa
  Building, 3F
2-2-1 Hirakawacho-cho
Chiyoda-ku, 102 Tokyo
Japan

The publication of *One Step at a Time, Intermediate 1* was directed by the members of the Newbury House Publishing Team at Heinle & Heinle:

Erik Gundersen, Editorial Director
John F. McHugh, Market Development Director
Kristin Thalheimer, Production Services Coordinator
Maryellen Eschmann Killeen, Production Editor
Amy Lawler, Managing Development Editor

Also participating in the publication of this program:
Publisher: Stanley J. Galek
Director of Production: Elizabeth Holthaus
Project Manager: Hockett Editorial Service
Senior Assistant Editor: Ken Pratt
Manufacturing Coordinator: Mary Beth Hennebury
Interior Designer and Compositor: Greta D. Sibley
Cover Designer: Gina Petti • Rotunda Design
Photo/Video Specialist: Jonathan Stark
Illustrator: Robert Holmes

Photo credits (page numbers appear in bold): Bob Daemmrich, Stock Boston—**53;** Michael Dwyer, Stock Boston—**157.**

Library of Congress Cataloging-in-Publication Data
Garcia, Judith.
    One step at a time.   Intermediate 1 / Judith D. Garcia.
       p.   cm.
    Summary : An introduction, intended for students who are not native English-speakers, to writing descriptive and process paragraphs.
     ISBN 0-8384-5030-X
     1. English language--Textbooks for foreign speakers. [1. English language--Textbooks for foreign speakers. 2. English language--Paragraphs.] I. Title.
    PE1128.G25   1995
  428.2'4--dc20
                                       95-46028
                                           CIP
                                         AC

Heinle & Heinle Publishers is a division of International Thomson Publishing, Inc.

Manufactured in the United States of America.

ISBN 0-8384-5030-X

10   9   8   7   6   5   4   3   2   1

Contents

CHAPTER THREE

The Conclusion 53

CHAPTER FOUR

Describing Personality Traits 77

CHAPTER FIVE

Describing Places and Objects .109

Preface

One Step at a Time, Intermediate 1 is the first of a two-level academic writing series for learners of English. It is a low intermediate writing text with accompanying skill-developing, interactive computer software programs for both the Windows and Macintosh platforms.

The complete *One Step at a Time* program has been developed to meet the needs of writing students at the low intermediate and intermediate levels and includes the following components:

- One Step at a Time, Intermediate 1
  - Text
  - Computerized interactive tutorials
    - Individual Macintosh package
    - Institutional Macintosh package
    - Macintosh demo
    - Individual Windows package
    - Institutional Windows package
    - Windows demo
- One Step at a Time, Intermediate 2
  - Text
  - Computerized interactive tutorials
    - Individual Macintosh package
    - Institutional Macintosh package
    - Macintosh demo
    - Individual Windows package
    - Institutional Windows package
    - Windows demo

The text is designed for a forty-hour course. It consists of seven chapters which take approximately five hours of classroom work each. The computerized interactive tutorials are thoroughly cross-referenced with the text and provide hours of additional practice.

OBJECTIVES OF *ONE STEP AT A TIME, INTERMEDIATE 1*

By the end of the course, the student will:

Plan and develop a paragraph with a topic sentence, body (containing major supports), and conclusion.
  a. Use appropriate paragraph form.
  b. Use logical organization.
  c. Write with clarity and coherence.

Write narrative and descriptive paragraphs using the following:
  a. Chronological sequence (process).
  b. Spatial sequence (in descriptions).

Write a variety of simple, compound, and complex sentences using coordinating conjunctions, subordinating conjunctions, and transitional words and expressions.
  a. Use parts of speech correctly.
  b. Use appropriate capitalization, punctuation, and spelling.
  c. Use correct word order.
  d. Edit sentences and paragraphs.

One Step at a Time, Intermediate 1 takes the student through the process of developing two types of narrative paragraphs: paragraphs that describe physical characteristics and personality traits, and paragraphs that describe a process. The introduction teaches the student the concepts of audience and purpose, academic writing versus nonacademic writing, and Standard American English. In early chapters, the student develops the ability to focus a topic, to select a controlling idea, and to write a topic sentence. S/he learns techniques such as brainstorming, listing, and concept mapping (clustering) to plan supporting ideas for a topic sentence. The importance of developing the controlling idea in each supporting sentence is stressed. Students learn to include controlling idea words as they work on concept maps and collaborative and individual writing tasks in each chapter. The student also learns to develop several kinds of conclusions to paragraphs.

The chapters of this text do not adhere to a rigid structure and may include from two to four sections depending on the content and objectives of the chapter. Each chapter of *One Step at a Time, Intermediate 1* guides the student through the basic grammatical structures and sentence patterns needed to create academic paragraphs of description and process. The chapters cover the basic grammatical structures, sentence patterns, and punctuation required to develop academic paragraphs. Much attention is given to the logical use and punctuation of coordinating conjunctions, subordinating conjunctions, and transitional words and expressions. While learning to develop paragraphs of description, students learn the basic parts of speech and how to avoid or correct fragments, run-on sentences, and comma splices. They also learn the correct placement of adjectives in sentences (after linking verbs and in noun phrases) and uses of pronoun and possessive adjectives, adverbs of frequency, and prepositional phrases. To create paragraphs of process, the student learns imperatives and modal auxiliaries, subordinating conjunctions of time and sequence, and transitional words commonly used in process paragraphs.

Each chapter contains individual and collaborative writing tasks which help students practice and internalize the writing, punctuation, and grammar concepts presented in the lessons. Most writing assignments are followed by in-class activities based on these assignments.

At the end of each chapter, the student completes a vocabulary building exercise, a journal assignment with a peer-editing follow-up activity, and a classroom feedback instrument for the teacher's use.

Appendices provide practice with present and present continuous tenses and topic sentences and also contain spelling, punctuation, and capitalization rules.

OBJECTIVES OF *ONE STEP AT A TIME, INTERMEDIATE 2*

Plan and develop a paragraph with a topic sentence, body (containing major and secondary supports) and conclusion.
   a. Use appropriate paragraph form.
   b. Use logical organization.
   c. Write with clarity and coherence.
   d. Use language appropriate to audience and purpose.

Write expository paragraphs using the following:
   a. Illustration and example.
   b. Classification.
   c. Comparison/contrast.
   d. Definition.

Write a variety of simple, compound and complex sentences.
   a. Use parts of speech correctly.
   b. Use appropriate capitalization, punctuation, and spelling.
   c. Use correct word order.
   d. Use appropriate transition words.
   e. Edit sentences and paragraphs.

The objectives of this text correlate with level four objectives on the Miami-Dade Community College ESL computerized placement test, the LEDA which will be available as part of the College Board Accuplacer 1996.

COMPUTERIZED INTERACTIVE TUTORIALS

Computerized interactive tutorials are provided as a supplement to the text's grammar objectives (present and present continuous tenses, adverbs of frequency, parts of speech and sentence building, sentence connecting, pronouns and possessive adjectives, adjectives in noun clauses). Interactive computer exercises are also provided to give students practice with such paragraph development skills as focusing topics, developing controlling ideas, and writing topic sentences. The computerized tutorials are thoroughly cross-referenced with the text; the computer disk logo indicates ideal times at which teachers and students might use the software.

Acknowledgments

Thanks to the five outstanding teachers I've had in my life. You all continue to be an inspiration! Joseph Edwards, David Durán, Tippe Schwabe, Janine Kreiter, and Walter Ricks.

Thanks to the people who gave their support and encouragement during this project: Rhonda Berger, director of the Instructional Technology Center at our college, for co-developing and designing the IBM software that accompanies both levels 1 and 2 of the textbook; the wonderful editors at Heinle & Heinle, Erik Gundersen and Amy Lawler, for their guidance and support; Rachel Youngman of Hockett Editorial Service for her expert management of the production process; Amy Rose for her precise copyediting; Greta Sibley for her wonderful design; Professor Stefanie Schinoff for her courage in piloting both the first version of the text and all of the beta versions of the software and for her helpful comments and suggestions for improvements in both; Sandra Koros and Professor Sharla Jones, for piloting (and debugging) much of the IBM software; Dr. Nestor Dominguez, my chairperson, for allowing the text and software to be piloted in our ESL program, and for believing that the use of technology in the classroom does enhance language learning; Midge Gives and Rosanne Roche for so cheerfully helping faculty use the "One Step at a Time" software in their computer labs; Dr. Kamala Anandam for agreeing to allow the text's IBM software to be adapted for use with Synergy's PSI Integrator.

Thanks to my professional colleagues who reviewed the manuscript at various stages throughout the developmental process and who offered many helpful suggestions for change:

- Wendy J. Allison, IELI, Hunter College, City University of New York

- Elizabeth Byleen, Applied English Center, University of Kansas

- Priscilla Eng, Middlesex Community College, Lowell, Massachusetts

- Pamela Friedman, Educational Consultant

- Kathy Keesler, Rio Hondo College

- Adrian Meerman, ELI, Queens College, City University of New York

- Elizabeth Mejía, IELI, Washington State University

- Lynne Nickerson, DeKalb College, Atlanta

- Karen Richelli-Kolbert, English Language Institute, Manhattanville College, New York

- Ann Roemer, Miami-Dade Community College, Wolfson Campus

- Cynthia Schuemann, Miami-Dade Community College, Wolfson Campus

- David Tillyer, City College, City University of New York

- Colleen Weldele, Palomar College, San Marcos, California

Thanks to my family: my daughters, Jenny and J. Michelle for their patience; my sisters, Georgina and Jennifer, for their encouragement; and my mother, Jeanette, for her love and support over the years.

And thanks to my students, without whom this book would have been neither possible nor necessary.

Introduction to Academic Writing

AUDIENCE AND PURPOSE

I write letters to my family to tell them how I am and to find out how they are.

I write notes to myself so I don't forget things.

There are different reasons why people write, and there are also many different styles of writing. People write notes, lists, directions, memos, and letters, and each of these has a different style with different sentence patterns, vocabulary, and tone. Directions and lists, for example, are not usually written in complete sentences. They do not have capital letters or punctuation. Letters and memos, on the other hand, usually use complete sentences and punctuation. Poetry frequently uses special "literary" styles such as uncommon sentence patterns, incomplete sentences, and no punctuation. There are three things, however, that all writing has in common. First, all writing has an author—the person who writes. Next, all writing has an audience—the person who is going to read the writing. (Sometimes the audience and the author are the same person.) Lastly, all writing also has a purpose—a reason the author is writing. These three elements, author, audience, and purpose, will determine what kind of sentence structure, vocabulary, and tone you use in your writing. You would not write the same note to your brother or sister that you would write to the president of your school, would you? The next few exercises will help you understand the concepts of "audience" and "purpose."

Class Discussion

Vocabulary

note	list	letter	memo	poem	story
complain	remember	request	explain	apologize	
inform	entertain	invite	communicate		

1. Why do people write? (Try to find as many "reasons" or "purposes" for writing as possible.)

   Look at the sentences at the top of this page, and then follow this example:

   I write ___letters___ to ___my parents___ when I need to ___ask them for money.___

   a. I write _____ to _____ when I

   need to _____ .

   b. I write _____ to _____ when I

   want to _____ .

   c. I write _____ to _____ when I

   have to _____ .

   d. I write _____ to _____ when I

   want to _____ .

2. Look at the two sentences at the top of page xii, and discuss these questions:
   a. How will the writing style in the letter to the family be different from the writing style in the note to myself?
   b. Why is the writing style in a letter different from the writing style of an informal note? In other words, what influences a person's writing style?
   c. Which style is better?[1]

3. What is an "audience"?

   An audience is a person or group of people who _____ .

4. When a person writes a love letter, the "audience" is the person who is going to receive that letter.

   Who is the "audience" for the list you make when you go to the market?

   Who is the "audience" for the notes you take in your classes?

   Who is the "audience" for the homework assignments that you turn in?

---

1 This is a trick question. Both of the styles are good IF they consider the audience and the purpose. All styles are valid IF they are used properly for the **audience** and **purpose** the writer intends. In other words, all writing must consider **the person/people who will be reading your writing** and **the reason for writing.** Remember this when you write and always ask yourself, "Why am I writing this?" and "Who will be reading this?"

5. Your writing style changes depending upon the person who will read what you write. Why do you think this happens?

Exercise Identify the audience and purpose of the following:

Example

>Sorry about last night. Why don't you come over? —I'll cook dinner

Author: a person who had a problem with somebody last night

Audience: a friend or family member that the author fought with

Purpose: to apologize and to invite the person to dinner

1.

>Nestor:
>
>Larry Wilson called at 3:00 re. some Salvadorian serpents. Call him back at 5:00. (305) 237-2000
>
>Cristi

Author: _____

Audience: _____

Purpose: _____

2.

>I would like to request a refund for this semester's tuition. I will be unable to attend classes here at Miami-Dade Community College because I am moving to Tallahassee. Thank you for your consideration.

Author: _____

Audience: _____

Purpose: _____

3.

> As bright as the stars shining in the sky
> over the Everglades on a moonless night—
> such is my love for you! Marry me!

Author: _____

Audience: _____

Purpose: _____

Paired Drill Discuss the following questions with a partner. Your partner covers side A; you cover side B. You ask question #1. Your partner should give you the answer that is in parentheses. If your partner has an answer that is very different from the one in parentheses, raise your hand and ask your professor if the answer was correct. Take turns asking the questions. Don't look at your partner's paper.

A	**B**
1. Who is the audience for a love letter? (a girlfriend or boyfriend; husband or wife)	1. Who is the audience for a grocery list? (the person who is going to the store)
2. Why do people write? (to communicate something to someone)	2. What does "audience" mean? (In writing, "audience" is the person/people who will read what you are writing.)
3. What does "purpose" mean? (Your "purpose" is your REASON for writing.)	3. When do you need to write academic paragraphs? (when you take a test or write a paper for a class or when you need to write reports at your work)
4. What kind of writing do you need to use if you want to impress an employer? (academic writing)	4. What kind of writing do you need to use if you remind yourself to buy milk? (informal or nonacademic writing— a list)

THE PURPOSE OF THIS TEXTBOOK

In this book, you will not develop many different styles of writing; no poetry or business letters, for example. You will write academic paragraphs, and your **audience** will be your teacher and at times your classmates. The types of sentences and the grammar you use for your paragraphs will be Standard American English,[2] which is the English that is used for academic, business, and professional audiences.

Your **purpose** in this textbook is to describe people, places, and objects, and to explain a process. This book will take you step by step through the process of writing these two different kinds of academic paragraphs: a description of a person, place, or thing; and a process that describes **how to do** something. You will begin by learning the (grammatical) elements you need to use to write simple sentences. Then you will learn to connect sentences and create compound and complex sentences. In each chapter, you will learn the step-by-step process that makes paragraph planning and writing easy.

Think: How can you use what you learn in this class later in life? In other words, when will you need to write academic paragraphs in the future?[3]

Discuss

1. What does all writing have in common (at least two aspects)?

2. What kind of writing will you learn in this class?

3. What is the purpose of most academic writing?

4. Who is the audience for your writing in this class?

5. Where will you be able to use what you learn in this class?

6. What do you think will be easy for you in this class?

7. What do you think will be difficult?

---

2 In academic writing, you must use Standard American English. There are many different dialects of English, but only one is accepted by the academic audience. This does not mean that these dialects are bad or wrong—it only means that they are different, and they are used for different audiences and different purposes.

3 You will need to write academic paragraphs if you plan to continue your college education after learning English. You will use the academic paragraph style on all of the major tests you take (TOEFL, MAPS, CLAST, GRE), as well as on all of the essay-style exams you take in your courses at college and later at any university. Scientific writing and business writing also use the academic style of writing.

WHAT WILL YOU LEARN IN THIS BOOK?

The first paragraphs you will write in this class will be descriptive paragraphs. You will learn to describe the physical characteristics and personality traits of people, as well as to describe places. To do this, you will learn to use all of the following:

- You may need to learn (or review) the **present** and **present continuous tenses** (also called present progressive) so you can begin writing complete sentences. The first appendix contains a complete review of these verb tenses.

- You will learn how to use **adverbs of frequency** (*sometimes, usually, never*) to explain how often things occur. Adverbs of frequency will help develop an interesting tone in your paragraphs that describe personality traits.

- You also need to learn to use **pronouns** (*I, me, you*) and **possessive adjectives** (*my, your, his*) so the reader knows exactly who or what you are writing about, and so your writing doesn't sound repetitive.

- To describe all of your topics, you will learn to use **adjectives** (*green, small, old*). They will tell your reader exactly how the objects in your paragraph look, feel, sound, taste, or smell, and your reader will be able to visualize the place, object, or person you are describing.

- **Prepositions of location** (*in, at, on*) and the expressions *there is/there are* will help you tell the location of the objects that you are describing.

- Then, to make your paragraph interesting and easy to read, you will need to learn how to use **sentence connectors.** When you connect sentences with words like *and, but, because, afterwards, therefore,* and *if,* your writing sounds fluent and sophisticated.

- At the same time that you learn these basic structures, you will also learn how to plan a paragraph using brainstorming and concept mapping techniques to focus a topic, develop controlling ideas, develop supporting details, and write conclusions.

As you can see, learning to write is a step-by-step process, and to write a descriptive paragraph, you need to know some basic structures. As you complete each chapter of the book, write down the new words you learned. Also, ask your teacher questions if there is anything you do not understand. There are computer software programs available for all of the above concepts, and they accompany this book. They will help you practice the skills you need to write correctly.

Introduction to Paragraph Development: The Topic Sentence

*I*n the first three chapters of this book, you will learn how to plan and write paragraphs to describe the physical characteristics of a person. The chapters will teach you how to do the following:

■ **STEP ONE**
Plan and write the topic sentence.

■ **STEP TWO**
Plan the support for the body of the paragraph.

■ **STEP THREE**
Plan and write the conclusion to the paragraph.

Warm-up Exercise

Write the affirmative form of the following verbs in the blanks in the following paragraph. Check to see that every verb agrees with its subject. Some blanks have more than one possible answer.

have(2)   **be(2)**   **look**   **seem**   **sense**

Mona Lisa _____ the most beautiful eyes in the world. They _____ large and brown with long lashes, and they have a beautiful almond shape. The expression in her eyes _____ soft and gentle, and sometimes it _____ mystical. When you _____ into Mona Lisa's eyes, you _____ the mystery and honesty of her feelings. Mona Lisa _____ the most expressive eyes I have ever seen.

Discussion   Look at the above paragraph and answer the following questions:

1. How many sentences are there in this paragraph? (Count the periods.)

   _____

2. How is the first line of the paragraph different from the other lines?

   _____

3. What is the topic of this paragraph (what does each sentence describe)?

   _____

4. What is the adjective that describes Mona Lisa's eyes in the first sentence?

   _____

5. Do all of the sentences in this paragraph make Mona Lisa's eyes sound "beautiful"?

   _____

6. List five words from the paragraph that make Mona Lisa's eyes sound "beautiful."

   _____

An academic paragraph of description usually has between five and eight sentences. It is indented about five spaces, and it looks like this:[1]

Topic sentence >. Body >. >. >. >. >. Conclusion >.

The paragraph on Mona Lisa's eyes is a good example of an academic paragraph of description. All academic paragraphs have three parts: a topic sentence, a body, and a conclusion.

THE TOPIC SENTENCE: OVERVIEW

Planning and writing the topic sentence involves three steps:

■ **STEP ONE**
Find and focus a topic.

■ **STEP TWO**
Think of a controlling idea.

■ **STEP THREE**
Write the focused topic and controlling idea as a complete sentence.

---

1 The supporting sentences in the paragraph may each have an additional sentence (called secondary support). You will learn to develop additional details as secondary support later in this book. For now, you will write only three supporting sentences for your topic sentence.

The **topic sentence** is usually the first sentence of an academic paragraph, and it is indented approximately five spaces. Remember these three rules about topic sentences:

1. The topic sentence has only one focused topic[2] (this names the person, place, or thing you are going to write about).

2. The topic sentence has only one controlling idea (this tells the reader what you will say about your focused topic).

3. The topic sentence must be written as a complete sentence.

STEP 1. FOCUSING THE TOPIC

In academic writing classes, the teacher often gives you the topic for your paragraphs, and you do not have to "focus" that topic, or make it more specific. All other times you can select your own topic for your academic writing. When you select your topic, you need to limit that topic so that you can write something meaningful and interesting about it in just one paragraph. If you do not **focus** your topic, your paragraph will be boring because it is too general; it will sound incomplete because you will leave out essential points in order to limit the size of your paragraph; or it will be too long because you try to put in all the essential details about a topic that is too big for one paragraph.

Learning to focus a topic is an important first step in learning to write concise academic paragraphs. The first step in learning to focus a topic is recognizing the difference between a general topic and a focused topic.

---

2 Except in paragraphs of comparison or contrast, in which two topics are necessary.

From General to Specific

Exercise 1.1 Notice that in this exercise your answer will be more specific than the general topic.

1. Give an example of a kind of dog.

   _____

2. Give the name of a famous author.

   _____

3. Give the name of a famous actor or actress.

   _____

4. Give an example of one mode of transportation.

   _____

5. Give the name of the most important political leader in your country today.

   _____

6. Give one aspect of living in this city that you find pleasant.

   _____

7. Give the name of an entertaining place that you like to visit in this city.

   _____

To focus a topic, you go from general to specific until there is ONE topic that you can describe in ONE paragraph. When you think that you have a good focused topic, you can check it. Just ask yourself, "Can I give three different examples or details about my topic, and will those three examples completely describe or explain what I want to say about my topic?" If the answer is "No," then continue to focus the topic until your answer is "Yes."

Look at the example below. You cannot write just one paragraph about all of the possible "methods of transportation" because the topic is too general. There are so many types of transportation in the world that you would have to write a book to discuss them all. Therefore, you need to focus the topic and find a more specific aspect (example) of "methods of transportation"—one aspect that can be developed with three supporting ideas:

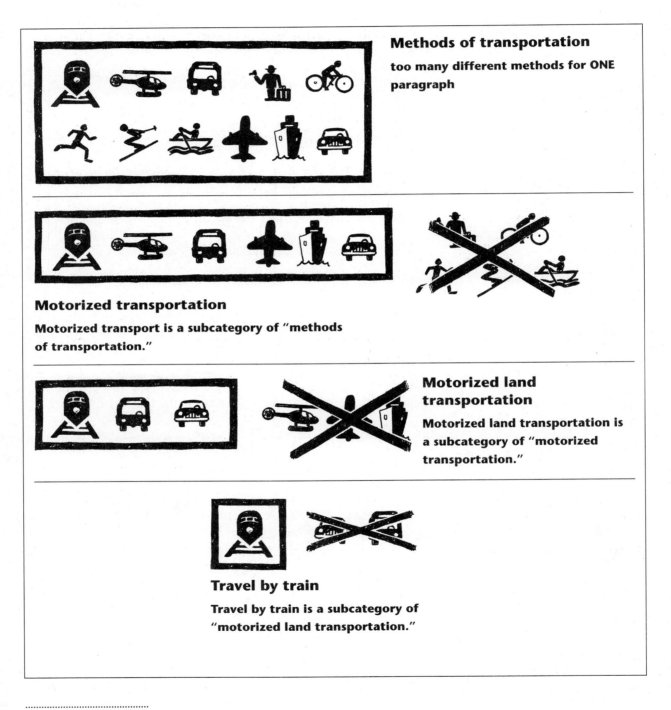

Methods of transportation

too many different methods for ONE paragraph

Motorized transportation

Motorized transport is a subcategory of "methods of transportation."

Motorized land transportation

Motorized land transportation is a subcategory of "motorized transportation."

Travel by train

Travel by train is a subcategory of "motorized land transportation."

Look at the following examples. In the first box, the focusing process is wrong. "My father" is not an example of "my mother." Also, "my sister" is not an example of "my uncle." The second box is focused correctly. Do you see how each new line is more specific than the one above it and also related to it?

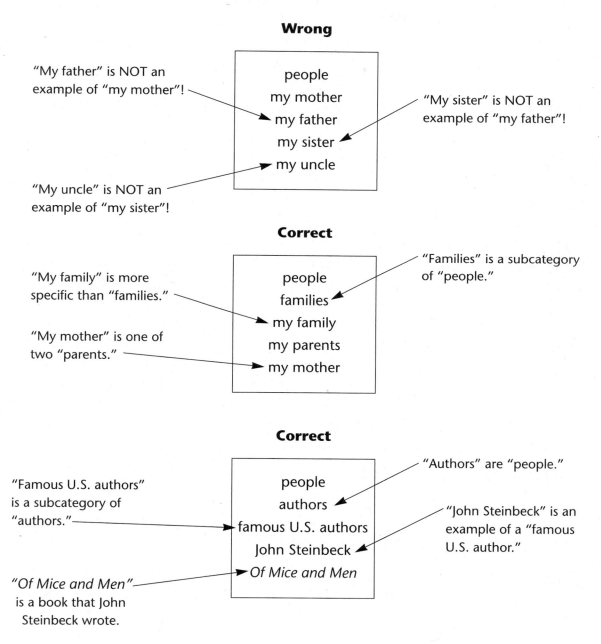

Wrong

"My father" is NOT an example of "my mother"!

people
my mother
my father
my sister
my uncle

"My sister" is NOT an example of "my father"!

"My uncle" is NOT an example of "my sister"!

Correct

"My family" is more specific than "families."

"My mother" is one of two "parents."

people
families
my family
my parents
my mother

"Families" is a subcategory of "people."

Correct

"Famous U.S. authors" is a subcategory of "authors."

"Of Mice and Men" is a book that John Steinbeck wrote.

people
authors
famous U.S. authors
John Steinbeck
Of Mice and Men

"Authors" are "people."

"John Steinbeck" is an example of a "famous U.S. author."

Exercise 1.2 Which of the items in the following focusing processes is wrong? Cross it out. Look at this example:

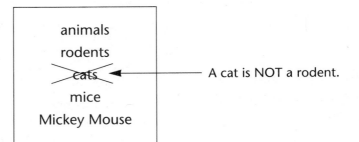

1.
animals
felines
cats
mice
Persian cats

2.
technology
computers
IBM computers
telephones
programming the IBM

3.
actors
American actors
comic American actors
comic French actors
Steve Martin

4.
animals
dogs
Dobermans
big dogs
my Doberman

5.
natural disasters
hurricanes
Hurricane Andrew
tornadoes

6.
famous people
famous authors
John Steinbeck
Nobel Prize–winning authors

Now fill in the missing focused topic:

7.
animals

domestic animals

_____

chickens

raising chickens

8.
books

academic books

_____

_____

the textbook for our
writing class

9.
food

American food

_____

_____

apple pie

Exercise 1.3 In the following exercise, you will put the topics in order according to how specific they are. The most general topic will be "1," the next most general will be "2," and so on. Follow the examples.

Examples

__2__ famous politicians in U.S. history   __4__ the Concorde

__4__ Abraham Lincoln   __2__ air transportation

__1__ famous people   __3__ large transcontinental jets

__3__ presidents of the U.S.   __1__ transportation

__5__ Abraham Lincoln's profile   __5__ buying a ticket to fly on the Concorde

1.

_____ teachers in the English program at this school

_____ teachers at this school

_____ writing teachers in the English program at this school

_____ people in education

_____ education

2.

_____ trees

_____ palm trees

_____ trees native to the tropics

_____ coconut palm trees

3.

_____ Gabriel García Márquez

_____ famous contemporary authors

_____ famous contemporary authors from Colombia

_____ famous authors

_____ famous people

4.

_____ women

_____ John's girlfriend

_____ John's girlfriend's face

_____ John's girlfriend's physical

_____ John's girlfriend's smile

Exercise 1.4 Focus the following topics. Each time you focus a topic, make sure that your new topic is more specific than (but directly related to) the topic above it. (You do not have to use all of the lines.)

1. People

famous people

famous politicians

famous U.S. politicians

President Clinton

Mr. Clinton's face

2. Plants

plants in the U.S.

Florida plants

the Ixora

care of Ixora

3. Television

_____

_____

_____

_____

4. Education

_____

_____

_____

_____

_____

5. Animals

_____

_____

_____

_____

_____

6. Actors

_____

_____

_____

_____

_____

7. Countries

_____

_____

_____

_____

_____

8. Professions

_____

_____

_____

_____

_____

Exercise 1.5 Focus the following topics for homework. (Notice that some are repeated from the previous exercise. Focus them again, but use different words.)

1. Actors

_____

_____

_____

_____

_____

2. Animals

_____

_____

_____

_____

_____

3. Singers

_____

_____

_____

_____

_____

4. Countries

_____

_____

_____

_____

_____

5. Education

_____

_____

_____

_____

_____

6. Technology

_____

_____

_____

_____

_____

7. Medicine

_____

_____

_____

_____

8. Money

_____

_____

_____

_____

STEP 2. SELECTING THE CONTROLLING IDEA

 The computer program that accompanies this section is called: "Controlling Ideas" (Macintosh and IBM)

Developing Controlling Ideas

After you focus the topic, the next step is to select a good controlling idea for your topic sentence. Remember that the controlling idea lets the reader know what you are going to say about your focused topic. It is probably the most important part of a paragraph of description, so select the best controlling idea possible. In the next section, you will learn a fun method for selecting controlling ideas.

Brainstorming and Concept Maps

Now you know the difference between general and focused topics, and you are ready to use the creative techniques of **brainstorming** and **concept mapping** to find a controlling idea and then to plan a descriptive paragraph.[3] Brainstorming means exploring a topic by writing down *every* thought that comes into your mind about that topic, even if you think the idea is silly or irrelevant. After you brainstorm, you choose only the best ideas from your list to begin your paragraph. Concept mapping (also called clustering) is one variation of brainstorming. In a concept map, you connect the ideas that you think of to other related ideas using a graphic system of circles and lines or arrows. On the following pages, you will use brainstorming and concept mapping to develop a controlling idea and plan a descriptive paragraph.

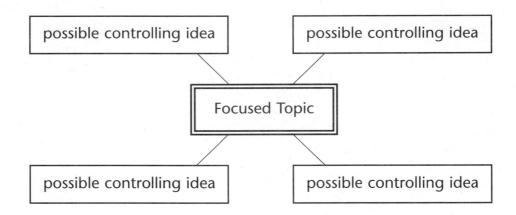

---

3 There are many different ways to plan paragraphs (listing, outlining, freewriting). As you advance through your study of English composition, you will learn a variety of planning techniques for your academic writing tasks. You will eventually find the one that you feel comfortable with. The method of planning that you use is up to you—the important thing is that you DO plan your paragraph before you begin writing it.

The following is a concept map that focuses the topic, "Mona."

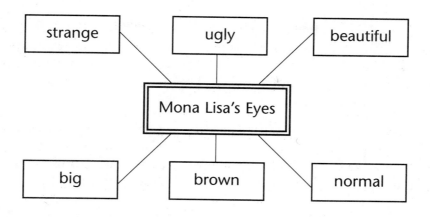

Now you need to select the best adjective from your concept map for your controlling idea. To do this, look for the most descriptive, general adjective you can find. You need to find an adjective that has many synonyms, so you can develop your supporting sentences without repeating the same word (controlling idea word) over and over. When you select your controlling idea, don't use words like *nice, good, bad, interesting, big, little,* and other adjectives that are not precise or that would be boring in a paragraph. Don't select a controlling idea that is too specific, such as *brown* or *large*. There would be nothing to develop in the paragraph.

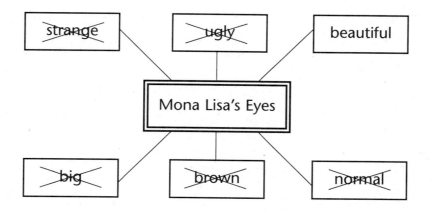

You can see from the paragraph below that the writer decided to describe the eyes' beauty. The writer combines the focused topic, *Mona Lisa's eyes,* and the controlling idea, *beautiful,* into one complete sentence. This sentence is called the **topic sentence.**

Mona Lisa has the most beautiful eyes in the world. They are large and brown with long lashes, and they have a beautiful almond shape. The expression in her eyes is soft and gentle, and sometimes it seems mystical. When you look into Mona Lisa's eyes, you sense the mystery and honesty of her feelings. Mona Lisa has the most expressive eyes I have ever seen.

The word "beautiful" in the first sentence is the controlling idea for the paragraph. Every sentence in the paragraph describes Mona Lisa's beautiful eyes. Of course, the focused topic, Mona's eyes, is essential because it tells the reader what you are going to talk about, but the controlling idea tells the reader precisely what it is that you are going to say about the topic.

Exercise 1.6 Brainstorm and draw concept maps to add a controlling idea to these focused topics:

```
┌─────────────────────┐
│  Abraham Lincoln    │
└─────────────────────┘
```

```
┌─────────────────────┐
│  the Bengal tiger   │
└─────────────────────┘
```

STEP 3. WRITING THE TOPIC SENTENCE

The next step is to combine the focused topic and the controlling idea into one complete sentence and thus to create your topic sentence. Your topic sentence should be one complete sentence[4] with a subject and a verb, and it should contain your focused topic and controlling idea.

Examples

CONTROLLING IDEA	FOCUSED TOPIC

Mona Lisa has **beautiful** **eyes.**

Mona Lisa's **smile** is **mysterious.**

FOCUSED TOPIC	CONTROLLING IDEA

CONTROLLING
IDEA

Mona Lisa has the most **famous smile** in the world.

FOCUSED
TOPIC

---

4 In this book, you will practice writing one-sentence topic sentences. As your writing courses become more advanced, you may learn how to develop two-sentence topic sentences, and to write paragraphs where the topic comes in the middle or at the end of the paragraph. Writing a one-sentence topic sentence is only the first step.

With a partner, write topic sentences with the words given below.

Example

Maria / smile / mysterious

Your topic sentence:

Maria has a mysterious smile.   *or*   Maria's smile is mysterious.

1. Karen / eyes / romantic

    Your topic sentence:

    _____

2. Rhonda / face / sweet

    Your topic sentence:

    _____

3. The expression on Jeanette's face / funny

    Your topic sentence:

    _____

4. Jordy / expression / silly

    Your topic sentence:

    _____

5. My instructor / expression / kind

    Your topic sentence:

    _____

Exercise 1.7 Write topic sentences for the following topics. Be sure to name the topic in the sentence:

Example

Your favorite classmate

_____ Marie Nock has a wonderful personality. _____

1. Your favorite classmate

_____

2. Your favorite politician

_____

3. Your favorite author

_____

4. Your favorite relative

_____

Exercise 1.8 Do this exercise with a partner on a separate piece of paper. Use the techniques you have just learned to write topic sentences for the following general topics. Make a list to focus your topic, and make a concept map to find a controlling idea. Then write one complete sentence with the focused topic and the controlling idea. Your sentence will be a topic sentence.

1. Animals
2. Poets
3. This city
4. Television programs
5. Food

6. People
7. Books
8. Relatives
9. Music
10. Weather

Exercise 1.9 With a partner, write topic sentences for the following pictures:

(1)   (2)   (3)

1. _____

2. _____

3. _____

TOPIC SENTENCE DO'S AND DON'T'S[5]

The computer program that accompanies this section is called: "Topic Sentence Don't's"

There are only three topic sentence "Do's" to remember when you write a topic sentence:

1. Focus your topic.

2. Choose an excellent controlling idea.

3. Write the focused topic and the controlling idea in one complete sentence.

It sounds easy, doesn't it? But there are ten common problems that students have when they are learning to write topic sentences. The following ten "Don't's" are rules you can use to check your topic sentence BEFORE you begin to develop your paragraph. The rules are explained in detail, along with exercises, in Appendix #2, "Topic Sentence Don't's."

---

5 The idiomatic expression "the do's and don't's" refers to any set of rules or advice to explain how to do and NOT to do something.

About the topic sentence in general:

Don't #1   Don't write a fragment as a topic sentence.

Don't #2   Don't "announce the topic."

Don't #3   Don't write the topic sentence as a personal opinion.

Don't #4   Don't put the paragraph's supporting ideas in the topic sentence.

About the focused topic:

Don't #5   Don't forget to focus the topic.

Don't #6   Don't write more than one focused topic.

Don't #7   Don't omit the topic.

About the controlling idea:

Don't #8   Don't omit the controlling idea.

Don't #9   Don't write more than one controlling idea.

Don't #10   Don't use vague words as controlling ideas.

VOCABULARY BUILDING

Write five new vocabulary words that you learned in class this week. Next to each word, write a synonym for the word (or the translation of the word in your own language if you cannot find a synonym). Then write the word in a sentence.

1. _____

_____

2. _____

_____

3. _____

_____

4. _____

_____

5. _____

_____

1. Do you like to write?   __ yes __ no

2. Did this lesson seem easy or difficult?   __ easy __ difficult

3. What was easy in this lesson?

   _____

4. What was difficult in this lesson?

   _____

5. Were there enough homework exercises for this unit?   __ yes __ no

6. Does your teacher explain the lesson clearly?   __ yes __ no

7. Does your teacher understand you?   __ yes __ no

8. Do you understand your teacher?   __ yes __ no

9. For which parts of this lesson would you like to have some more exercises?

   _____

chapter two

The Body of the Paragraph: Describing People (Physical Characteristics)

■ **STEP ONE**
Decide on three supporting ideas (aspects).

■ **STEP TWO**
Plan the development of the controlling idea (synonyms).

■ **STEP THREE**
Write the supporting ideas in complete sentences.

STEP 1. DECIDING ON THREE SUPPORTING IDEAS

Now that you have your topic sentence, the next step is to plan the supporting ideas that develop the topic sentence. These supporting sentences are called the **body** of the paragraph. A paragraph of description needs three major supporting ideas (developed in three to six sentences)[1] in the body. Each supporting idea must do two things: It must describe an aspect of the topic, and it must develop the topic's controlling idea. The three aspects that the Mona Lisa paragraph describes are the expression of her eyes, their shape, and the influence they have on the person who looks at them. In the body of the paragraph, these three aspects of Mona Lisa's eyes must be described as "beautiful," the controlling idea.

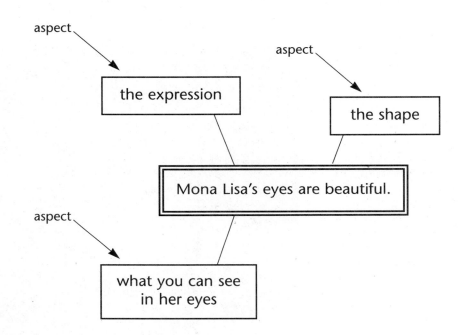

Look at the following three concept maps. They are used to plan the particular **aspects** that the writer is going to develop in the main supporting sentences. The controlling ideas are not added to the supporting details in the concept map yet, because first the writer must decide what three aspects of the topic to describe. Can you think of some adjectives that would develop the controlling idea in each concept map?

---

1 This means that your paragraphs will probably have between five and eight sentences. Later you will learn how to add more details to each of these three sentences to create "secondary support," and your paragraphs may be longer.

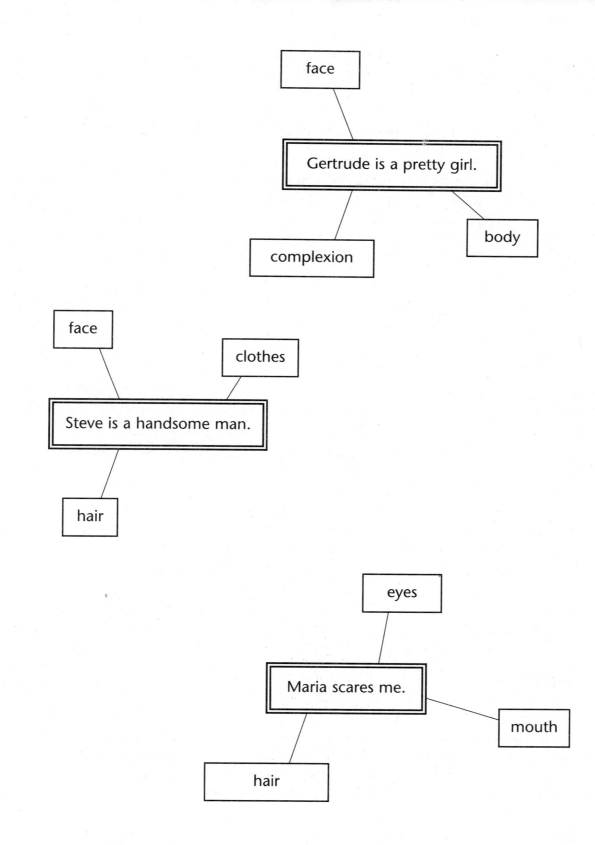

STEP 2. PLANNING THE DEVELOPMENT OF THE CONTROLLING IDEA

The computer program that accompanies this section is called: "Controlling Ideas" (Macintosh and IBM)

You can use the concept mapping technique to think of three supporting ideas for the body of your paragraph. Then you can add the details to them. These details will be synonyms of your controlling idea. For example, if your controlling idea is "ugly," all of the sentences in your paragraph will show how the subject of your paragraph is "ugly." This is what the concept map for the paragraph on Mona Lisa looked like:

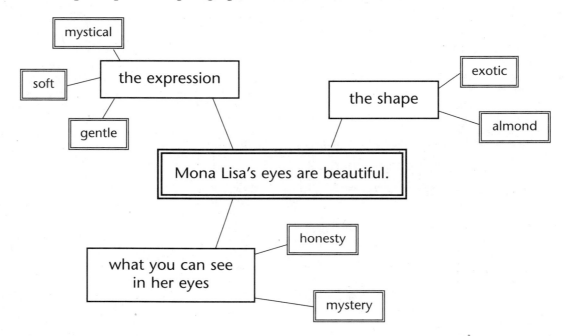

The writer of this paragraph describes beauty in Mona Lisa's expression, the shape of the eyes, and the impression people get when they look at her. Each supporting sentence contains adjectives and expressions that develop the controlling idea, "beautiful."

Exercise 2.1 Look again at the paragraph about Mona Lisa. Circle all the words that develop the controlling ideas.

Mona Lisa has the most beautiful eyes in the world. They are large and brown with long lashes, and they have a beautiful almond shape. The expression in her eyes is soft and gentle, and sometimes it seems mystical. When you look into Mona Lisa's eyes, you sense the mystery and honesty of her feelings. Mona Lisa has the most expressive eyes I have ever seen.

Exercise 2.2 Sit with a partner for this exercise. Look at the topic sentences in the boxes below, and identify which sentences develop the controlling idea of that topic sentence. Write "Y" in the blank to the left of the sentence if the sentence will develop the controlling idea in the topic sentence. Write "N" in the blank if the sentence will NOT develop the controlling idea. Underline the words you and your partner do not understand, and then use a dictionary to look up the words.

Henry Jameson has a funny face.

Y / N

__ 1. His small eyes are crossed.

__ 2. He collects frogs.

__ 3. His nose is so tiny that it looks like a button with two holes in it.

__ 4. His mouth is always smiling and happy.

__ 5. His chin is almost nonexistent.

__ 6. He has a million freckles on his comical face.

__ 7. His face is always clean.

__ 8. I like Henry's personality.

__ 9. Henry studies with me.

__ 10. His thin red hair sticks out all over his head.

(Optional: Can you draw a picture of Henry Jameson? Use a separate piece of paper.)

When Jennifer is happy, everyone who sees her face feels happy, too.

Y / N

__ 1. Her impish green eyes light up when she smiles.

__ 2. She has a wide cheerful smile that delights people.

__ 3. She has long brown hair.

___ 4. Her eyes crinkle and shine with happiness.

___ 5. She likes animals.

___ 6. Her soft bubbly laughter makes those around her smile.

___ 7. She has a cat named Bufferin.

___ 8. She has a sunny expression on her face.

___ 9. She is popular where she works.

___ 10. She lives in California.

(Optional: Can you draw a picture of Jennifer? Use a separate piece of paper.)

Exercise 2.3 With a partner, add details to the following concept maps that will develop the controlling idea for each topic sentence.

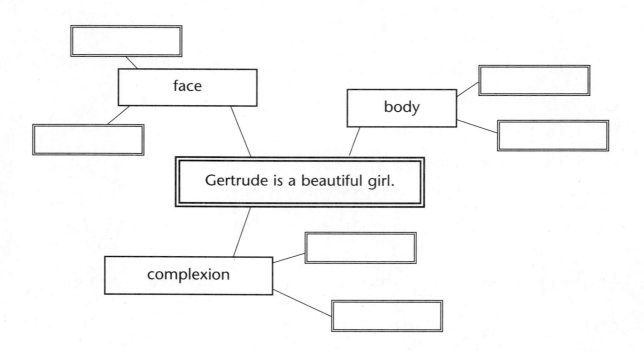

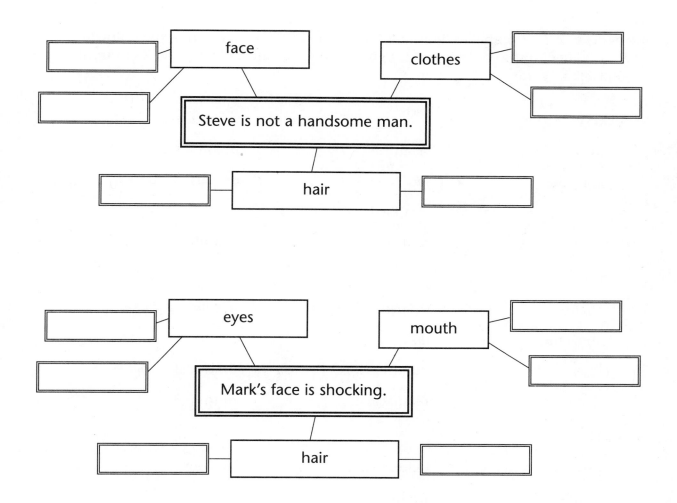

Exercise 2.4 With your partner or as a class, choose one of the concept maps from above and write a paragraph using the information in it.

_____

_____

_____

_____

_____

_____

_____

Exercise 2.5 Vocabulary building (dictionary exercise): Which of the following words is NOT related to the controlling idea given above the choices? Put an "X" in front of the UNRELATED words.

Pretty

__ wonderful	__ beautiful	__ frightening
__ gorgeous	__ sad	__ dreamy
__ hideous	__ wrinkled	__ exotic
__ ugly	__ homely	__ charming

Crazy

__ smart	__ flipped	__ peculiar
__ shocking	__ daft	__ insane
__ loco	__ handsome	__ irrational
__ demented	__ maniacal	__ funny

Ugly

__ pretty	__ deformed	__ hideous
__ homely	__ frightful	__ grotesque
__ handsome	__ offensive	__ unsightly
__ terrifying	__ repulsive	__ unattractive

Comfortable

__ cheery	__ cozy	__ hard
__ cold	__ odd	__ restful
__ homey	__ homely	__ pleasing
__ quiet	__ noisy	__ warm

Exercise 2.6 Circle all of the adjectives that make Martha look "strange" in this paragraph.

Martha is the strangest-looking friend that I have. She has long stringy red hair, and she never brushes it, so it always flies around her head in all directions and looks wild. In addition, even though Martha needs to wear her glasses all the time, she usually forgets to put them on, and she squints, which makes her look worried. Finally, her mouth is unusual because she has very thin lips and large teeth, so when she smiles, it looks like she is growling. Martha is a strange-looking girl, and many people think she is not very pretty, but she is my friend and, in my opinion, her wonderful personality makes up for her strange appearance.

(Optional: Draw a picture of Martha on a separate piece of paper. Change some of the details of her face, and then describe the changes to a classmate.)

Exercise 2.7 In the paragraphs below, the writer did not use the controlling idea at all in the paragraph. With a partner, underline the adjectives that do not mean the same as the controlling ideas in the topic sentences. Then change the incorrect words for adjectives that develop the controlling ideas. (The conclusions are correct, so don't change them.) Rewrite each paragraph.

My father has a handsome face. His eyes and complexion are not very attractive. He has deep brown eyes and a medium dark complexion. He has ugly hair, too. His soft wavy hair and his eyebrows are black. His mouth is ugly. He has a medium-size mouth, but his teeth are not straight, and they are yellow. He also has a ridiculous little moustache. I love my father's face. I am glad that I look like him.

_____

_____

_____

_____

_____

_____

_____

_____

_____

Some people think that my father has an ugly head. It makes him look noble and kind. His head is very small and round like a ball, and he has only a little thin reddish hair around the bottom of his head. I love the way his head looks. The center of his head is bald, and on the bald part of my father's head there are large brown spots. I suppose that my father does have an ugly head; however, he also has a big heart and a wonderful personality, and I love him very much.

_____

_____

_____

_____

_____

_____

_____

_____

_____

Exercise 2.8 Look at the picture below, and fill in the details of the concept map using any of the adjectives below, or use a dictionary and find adjectives that develop the idea of "scary."

ugly	crooked	evil
toothless	hideous	scary
terrifying	frightening	
cruel	wicked	bad

When you have finished your concept map, write the supporting sentences for the paragraph.

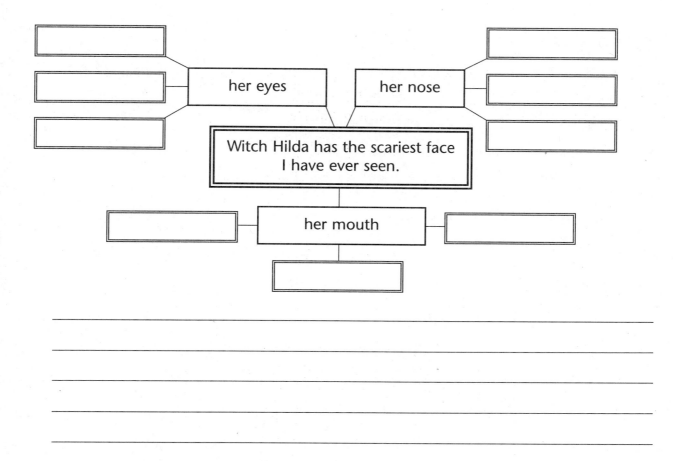

Witch Hilda has the scariest face I have ever seen.

her eyes

her nose

her mouth

STEP 3. WRITING THE SUPPORTING IDEAS IN COMPLETE SENTENCES

The computer program that accompanies this section is called: "Building Sentences" (Macintosh) and "Complete Sentences—Fragments and Run-Ons" (IBM)

Sentences and Fragments

   In this part of the chapter, you will learn about simple sentences and about three problems you should avoid when you write sentences: (1) fragments, (2) run-on sentences, and (3) comma splices.

   A complete sentence (simple sentence) has a subject, a verb, and sometimes a direct or an indirect object. A sentence expresses a complete idea. A complete sentence is also called an "independent clause." Let's look at the different parts of an independent clause now, starting with subjects.

Subjects

The **subject** of the sentence is usually the performer of the action or the person or thing being described. The subject can be a noun or a pronoun.

Examples   Subjects appear in **boldfaced** type.

He is going to be home late tomorrow.

Is **John** going to be home late tomorrow?

This class is very exciting, isn't **it?**

My mother loves me very much.

Where are **you** going?

Exercise 2.9   Fill in the blank with an appropriate subject.

1. _____ is my best friend.

2. Frequently, _____ comes late to class.

3. My teacher likes me because _____ am a good student.

4. Is _____ absent today?

5. _____ studies a lot.

Verbs

The **verb** in the sentence usually shows action *(run, smile, study)*. It can also show exis-tence *(be)* or a state *(seem, look, smell)*. The verb also tells the time of the action; for example, past tense tells of something that happened in the past; simple present tense tells of habit-ual or repeated action.

Examples   Verbs appear in **boldfaced** type.

My sister **helps** my mother every week

Carolyn Ortega **is** a wonderful teacher.

Does the sandwich **taste** good?

There **are** not enough chairs here for all of us.

Exercise 2.10   Fill in the blank with an appropriate verb.

1. I _____ every day.

2. My best friend _____ every day.

3. The teacher never _____ .

Direct and Indirect Objects

Some verbs, called **transitive verbs,** transfer action from subject to object, and they are always followed by an object.

Examples   Transitive verbs appear in **boldfaced** type.

I **hit** the ball.

"Hit" is transitive and must be followed by a direct object *(the ball)*.

We **gave** the letter to them.

"Give" is transitive and must be followed by a direct object *(the letter)* and an indirect object *(to them)*.

If you use a direct object and an indirect object in the sentence, there are two rules you must remember.

RULES

1. When the indirect object comes **after** the direct object, you must use "to" (or "for").

2. When the indirect object comes **before** the direct object, do NOT use "to."

Examples

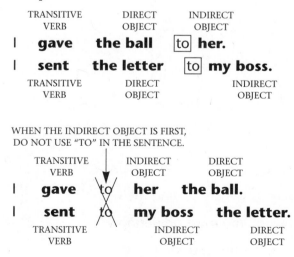

The waiter gave **the lemonade to Jack.**
DIRECT   INDIRECT
OBJECT   OBJECT

The waiter gave **Jack the lemonade.**
INDIRECT   DIRECT
OBJECT   OBJECT

Exercise 2.11 Fill in the blank with an appropriate object. Use pronouns for names of people.

Examples

We are going to send ___him___ the ___letter___ .

We are going to send ___the letter___ to ___him___ .

1. I need to give _____ to _____ .

2. I need to give _____ the _____ .

3. You must give all of the _____ to

   _____ if you want a good grade.

4. Did you mail the _____ to _____ ?

5. Did you mail _____ the _____ ?

6. Please give _____ the _____ .

7. Did you send the _____ to _____ ?

● Intransitive Verbs

Other verbs do *not* need direct objects. They are called **intransitive verbs.**

Examples

1. The baby is sleeping.   **wrong:** I'm sleeping the baby.

2. We are staying for a week.   **wrong:** We are staying them.

3. You must go now.   **wrong:** You must go her now.

4. They are coming here tonight.   **wrong:** They are coming us.

Exercise 2.12   Use these words in complete sentences.

1. my uncle / travel / Europe / in the summer

_____

2. brother / wake up / late / Saturdays

_____

3. they / leave / early

_____

4. the ship / be / large

_____

● Imperatives

The imperative (or command form) does not require a subject. Commands are complete sentences. This is because the only possible subject for an imperative sentence is "you"!

Affirmative:	**Negative:**
Come in.	Please don't come in.
Please sit down.	Don't sit down.
Do this now, please.	Please don't do this now.

Exercise 2.13   Sit with a classmate, and write three commands (affirmative) for any of your classmates.

Example

Juan, please speak only English in the class.

1. _____

2. _____

3. _____

Exercise 2.14 Now write three commands (negative) for your classmates.

Example

Marcelle, please don't laugh when I try to speak English in class.

1. _____

2. _____

3. _____

● Complete Sentences and Fragments

Exercise 2.15 The following are complete sentences. Underline the subjects and circle the verbs:

Example

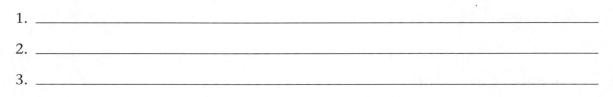

Joe (ate) canned tuna for dinner.

1. This is nice.

2. Stop it.

3. The baby is sleeping quietly.

4. Marsha studied.

5. After Mark graduated from college, he got a job at the United Nations.

6. She will be a wonderful mother.

7. Do you understand this now?

Exercise 2.16 The following are NOT complete sentences. They are **fragments,** and they are not correct. A fragment needs a subject, a verb, or an object to become a complete and correct sentence. Make each fragment into a sentence. Then underline the subjects and circle the verbs.

Example

Nancy and her husband, that man over there with the yellow hat

Nancy and her husband, that man over there with the yellow hat, (are speaking) with my uncle.

1. Came to class in the morning

_____

2. Is a nice day today

_____

3. Sally sends

_____

4. Studies at the college in the afternoon

_____

5. Italian classes here the Miami-Dade Community College

_____

Drill Indicate which of the following sentences are fragments and which are complete sentences. Fix the fragments.

S / F

___   1. Albert Einstein was born in 1879.

_____

___   2. Please don't give tomorrow.

_____

___   3. The weather in Canada in January, February, and March.

_____

___   4. I'm just trying to give.

_____

___   5. Is 3:00 and is a sunny day.

_____

___   6. You and I trying to buy the same sweater.

_____

___ 7. Studying at the college to get a good job.

_____

___ 8. My uncle's favorite actor, Dustin Hoffman.

_____

___ 9. Opens Friday at theaters everywhere.

_____

___ 10. Do you understand this concept now?

_____

___ 11. Who you talking to?

_____

___ 12. Please come in and sit down.

_____

___ 13. Will you please send tomorrow?

_____

___ 14. Felt it was important to talk about family values.

_____

___ 15. Children often grow up in nonconventional families.

_____

● Run-ons and Comma Splices

When two complete independent sentences are written as one sentence, without end punctuation,[2] the sentence is called a **run-on sentence.** It is NOT correct. When the independent sentences are separated only by a comma with no connecting words, it is called a **comma splice.** These are ERRORS in writing. Look at these sentences (they are WRONG).

_____

2 Period, question mark, or exclamation point.

wrong:

COMMA SPLICE

Jerry is **here, his** brother is absent.

Jerry is **here his** brother is absent.
RUN-ON

wrong:

COMMA SPLICE

It is raining **today, it** will probably be sunny tomorrow.

It is raining **today it** will probably be sunny tomorrow.
RUN-ON

There are several ways to fix a run-on sentence, and we will study several of them in this book. One way to correct a run-on or comma splice is to separate the two independent clauses with a period.

wrong: Jerry is here his brother is absent

correct: Jerry is **here. His** brother is absent.

wrong: It is raining today, it will probably be sunny tomorrow.

correct: It is raining **today. It** will probably be sunny tomorrow.

Exercise 2.17 Use periods to correct the run-on sentences and comma splices in this paragraph.

I came to the United States in January of 1988 I went to Killian Senior High School, I finished eleventh grade, I took my GED because I needed to go to California, I couldn't take time off from school I returned to Miami, I stayed here a few months then I went to Nicaragua on vacation, after two months, I came back to Miami I went back to school for English classes.

_____

_____

_____

_____

_____

_____

_____

Exercise 2.18 Use periods to correct the run-on sentences and comma splices.

1. Pat has a homely face she has a huge crooked nose the expression in her eyes is usually cold and cruel her mouth is small.

   _____

   _____

2. Augusto arrived here from Guatemala two years ago, he came to this country for personal reasons now he wants to earn lots of money.

   _____

   _____

3. My husband has a beautiful face he has gentle blue eyes with long lashes, his hair is soft his eyebrows are arched, his nose is straight.

   _____

   _____

4. Pilar is a very good student, she studies hard every day two or three hours, she likes to spend a lot of time analyzing her homework and tests from class.

   _____

   _____

5. My 15-year-old niece, Olga, is an active girl, she is studying in a special English music and humanities school in Odessa she has English and singing classes every day.

   _____

   _____

CONNECTING COMPLETE AND INCOMPLETE SENTENCES: COORDINATING CONJUNCTIONS

Using *and* to Connect Parts of Sentences

You can use the coordinating conjunction *and* to combine parts of sentences or complete sentences. Let's look first at how you can connect **parts of sentences** with *and*.

If you have only two words to connect (nouns, verbs, adjectives, etc.), you do not need a comma before *and*. If you have more than two nouns, you need a comma in front of *and*.[3]

You can use *and* to connect **nouns.**

> *My brother* **and** *my sisters* live in California.

> *My brother, my sisters,* **and** *my mother* live in California.

You can use *and* to connect **verbs.**

> I love to *swim* **and** *exercise.*

> I love to *swim, exercise,* **and** *jog.*

You can use *and* to connect **adjectives** after a noun.

> Sheila is *smart* **and** *pretty.*

> Sheila is *smart, rich, pretty,* **and** *intelligent.*

You can use *and* to connect **adverbs.**

> Professor Hauser speaks *clearly* **and** *loudly.*

> Professor Hauser speaks *clearly, loudly,* **and** *fast.*

You can use *and* to connect **objects.**

> I saw *Mark* **and** *John* at the conference last year.

> I saw *Mark, John,* **and** *Steve* at the conference last year.

You can use *and* to connect **prepositional phrases.** (The same rule for commas applies to all these uses.)

> My brother studied forestry *at Humboldt State University* **and** *at the University of California.*

> My brother studied forestry *at Humboldt State University, at the University of California,* **and** *at Stanford.*

---

3 The comma before *and* in a list is optional but is often used to avoid confusion.

Using Coordinating Conjunctions

The computer program that accompanies this section is called: "Connecting Sentences" (Macintosh and IBM)

And, but, so, for, yet, or, and *nor* are the coordinating conjunctions. You can use coordinating conjunctions to avoid (or correct) a run-on sentence. Coordinating conjunctions connect ideas and show the logical relationship between them. In this chapter, you will study *and, but,* and *so.* Observe how the meaning changes when the coordinating conjunction changes in the following examples:

I like Mary's car. It is a Neptune.

Mary's new car is a Neptune, **and** I like it. = **(two related facts about the car)**

Mary's new car is a Neptune, **but** I like it. = **(I don't usually like Neptunes.)**

Mary's new car is a Neptune, **so** I like it. = **(I like all Neptunes.)**

● *And*

Use *and* to connect complete sentences that are similar or parallel in meaning. Often the second sentence gives additional information about the first sentence.

Examples

John is an accountant, **and** Steven is a lawyer.

John went to Paris on his vacation, **and** Steven went with him.

To connect complete sentences with *and,* you need to remember two rules:

1. If you are joining two complete sentences (independent clauses), you need to put a comma in front of *and.*[4]

Examples

Jeanette Wilt won a prize for her poetry in 1985, **and** she called her family to tell them about it.

Georgina works in a hospital in Arcata, **and** her husband, Jim, is a real estate appraiser.

---

4 When the two sentences are very short, this comma is optional.

2. If you are joining sentences, and the second sentence is NOT a complete sentence (maybe it doesn't have a subject or a verb), then you do not use a comma in front of *and*.

Examples

Jennifer and Lee own a fishing boat **and go** out on the ocean at least once a week.

Jerry and Luanne are married **and live** in Fortuna.

Exercise 2.19 Add commas in any blanks where necessary.

1. The fires and earthquakes in California destroyed many houses __ and __ killed several people.

2. Bring your books __ and __ we can study together.

3. Computers help students learn quickly __ and __ they help teachers teach different things to students at the same time.

4. DoWan Kim is from Seoul, Korea. He is 21 __ and __ is single.

5. We are both from the same country __ and __ we are friends.

6. Most of my classmates come from South America __ and __ they speak Spanish.

7. I want to get married __ and __ buy my own home as soon as possible.

8. The day of the final exam, I was in the hospital with my sister __ and __ my mother.

9. I visited my sister for three hours __ and __ then I had to drive home at 2 AM.

10. Her son studies at Royal Green Elementary __ and __ her daughter studies at Sunset High School.

Exercise 2.20 Combine the following sentences using *and*.

Example

Idania lives in Kendall with her husband.

Idania lives in Kendall with her children.

Idania lives in Kendall with her brother.

Possible answers:

Idania lives in Kendall with her husband, children, and brother. **(best answer)**

Idania lives in Kendall with her husband, her children, and her brother.

Idania lives in Kendall with her husband, with her children, and with her brother.

1. Ana María's house is small. / Ana María's car is small. / Ana María's boat is small.

   _____

2. Lissett works 20 hours per week. / Lissett studies 30 hours per week.

   _____

3. Ana María lives in Fountainbleau. / Ana María studies at the Sorbonne. / Ana María works in a hospital.

   _____

4. I went to Havana when I was 18 years old. / I studied history and sociology.

   _____

5. Jaime likes to play racquetball in the park. / Jaime likes to work out in the gym. / Jaime likes to swim in the lake.

   _____

Exercise 2.21   Interview a classmate, and let the classmate interview you. Find out about hobbies, favorite movies, favorite authors, favorite foods, favorite places to go in this city, family members, plans for the future, and reason(s) for coming to this country. Make a list of your answers here:

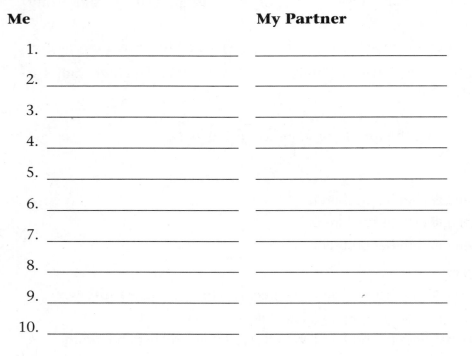

Me   **My Partner**

1. _____   _____

2. _____   _____

3. _____   _____

4. _____   _____

5. _____   _____

6. _____   _____

7. _____   _____

8. _____   _____

9. _____   _____

10. _____   _____

Now write three sentences using the SIMILARITIES you share with your partner. Use *and* in each sentence.

Example

Juan and I like to go to the beach, **and** we like to travel.

1. _____

   _____

2. _____

   _____

3. _____

   _____

● *But* to Connect Sentences

The coordinating conjunction *but* follows the same rules of punctuation as *and*. It is used to show contrast or surprise. When you use *but*, remember that the idea after *but* must be different from (or a contrast to) the idea(s) in the first part of the sentence.

Examples

Richard is poor, **but** he owns an extremely expensive car. **(comma)**

Richard is poor **but** owns an extremely expensive car. **(no comma)**

In this sentence, *but* means that it is surprising for a poor man to have an expensive car.

Exercise 2.22 Add *and* or *but* to connect each pair of sentences. Put commas where necessary.

1. It may be a bad idea _____ I am not coming to class tomorrow.

2. Tomorrow is Saturday _____ I am going to the museum.

3. This year is an election year _____ I am too young to vote.

4. I am too young to vote _____ I want Jones to win.

Combine the following sentences using either *and* or *but*.

5. Smith quit campaigning at the beginning of this election. / Now he is beginning to campaign again.

   _____

   _____

6. I know it is dangerous to swim alone. / I am going to do it anyway because my friends only want to play volleyball.

   _____

   _____

7. I love to go canoeing at Yosemite. / I love to go hiking at Shasta.

   _____

   _____

8. My brother loves to go hiking in the Avila Mountain of Caracas. / My brother hates canoeing on the Orinoco.

   _____

   _____

9. This exam is not easy. / I think I know all the answers.

   _____

   _____

10. Gabriel called me yesterday. / I didn't call him back.

   _____

   _____

Exercise 2.23 Using the details from your interview with a classmate on page 44 (Exercise 2.21), write three sentences that show DIFFERENCES between you and your partner.

Example

Juan came to this country for political reasons, **but** I came here because my wife's family lives in this country.

1. _____

_____

2. _____

_____

3. _____

_____

• *So to Connect Sentences*

When you use *so*[5] as a coordinating conjunction, write a complete sentence after it and put a comma in front of *so*. The sentence after *so* gives a RESULT.

Example

Jane has a headache, **so** she is going to take some aspirin.

(IN THIS SENTENCE, "THE HEADACHE" IS THE REASON OR CAUSE FOR JANE'S "TAKING ASPIRIN.")

wrong: I have a headache, **so am** going to stay home today.

(ERROR = NO SUBJECT AFTER *SO*)

correct: I have a headache, so **I** am going to stay home today.

wrong: The fire is heading for our house so we must evacuate.

(ERROR = NO COMMA IN FRONT OF *SO*)

correct: The fire is heading for our house, so we must evacuate.

Exercise 2.24 Add *and, but,* or *so* to connect these sentences. Put commas where necessary.

1. I have a cold _____ I am not going to school.

2. The tea is very hot _____ I have to drink it anyway because I am in a hurry to leave.

3. The dog is barking _____ somebody is probably at the door.

4. The sun is shining _____ the birds are singing. It is a beautiful day.

---

5 When the word *so* is used as a coordinating conjunction, it means "this is why" or "for this reason."

Combine the following sentences using either *and, but,* or *so.*

5. I studied very hard for this exam. / I failed this exam.

   _____

6. I didn't study hard for this exam. / I passed it.

   _____

7. I studied very hard for this exam. / I passed it.

   _____

8. This exam is difficult. / Many students are going to fail it.

   _____

Use these words to create sentences. Use *and, but,* or *so* in each sentence.

9. Jennifer / win / scholarship / she / not / go / UC Davis next year

   _____

10. Jim / have / vacation / go / Orlando / with / family

    _____

11. dog / smell / bad / give / it / bath

    _____

12. zoo / museum / closed / Monday

    _____

13. I / sleepy / not / go / bed

    _____

Complete these sentences logically.

14. I am in love with you, but _____.

15. I am in love with you, so _____.

16. I am in love with you, and _____.

17. The weather looks bad, but _____ .

18. The weather looks bad, so _____ .

19. The weather looks bad, and _____ .

20. He didn't pass the course, but _____ .

21. He didn't study that chapter, and _____ .

22. He didn't study this chapter, so _____ .

Exercise 2.25 Combine each set of sentences using *and, but,* or *so.*

1. Julio is my classmate. / He is my friend.

   _____

   _____

2. Pietro lives in Rome. / He doesn't work at the Vatican.

   _____

   _____

3. June works full time. / She studies full time.

   _____

   _____

4. Marsha wants to improve her English. / She studies English at night at Eureka City Schools.

   _____

   _____

5. Kevin is a healthy boy. / He has the flu. / He doesn't feel well today.

   _____

   _____

Exercise 2.26 Using the details from your interview with a classmate on page 44, write two sentences that show RESULTS.

Example

Juan and I like to read books by Gabriel García Márquez, so I am going to lend him my copy of *One Hundred Years of Solitude.*

1. _____

   _____

2. _____

   _____

Exercise 2.27 Take one of your homework or journal paragraphs and rewrite it on a separate piece of paper. Be sure your paragraph has a controlling idea. Use *and, but,* and *so* in your paragraph. To do this, you will probably need to add more ideas to the supporting sentences.

Exercise 2.28 Look at the picture below. On a separate piece of paper, write ten sentences (not a paragraph) about this busy family's day at the park. Use *and, but,* or *so* in each sentence. Then exchange papers with a classmate and try to find any mistakes in punctuation. Pay particular attention to sentences with *and, but,* and *so.*

Write ten new vocabulary words that you learned in class this week. Next to each word, write the translation for the word in your own language. Then write the word in a sentence.

1. _____

   _____

2. _____

   _____

3. _____

   _____

4. _____

   _____

5. _____

   _____

6. _____

   _____

7. _____

   _____

8. _____

   _____

9. _____

   _____

10. _____

    _____

1. I did my homework last week.

   __ yes   It took _____ minutes each night.

   __ no   because _____

2. I came to class on time all week.

   __ yes

   __ no   because _____

3. I understand my teacher and classmates

   __ 20% of the time.   __ 50% of the time.   __ all the time.

4. Would you recommend this class and teacher to other students? Why? Why not?

   _____

5. What did YOU contribute to the class today?

   _____

6. What could you have done better to prepare for today's class?

   _____

7. How do you feel when you write in English? Is it easy for you? Difficult? Why?

   _____

8. If you did the computer program that accompanies this chapter, did it help?

   _____

9. List three new things that you learned this week in this class.

   _____

chapter three

The Conclusion

■ **STEP ONE**
Restates the focused topic.

■ **STEP TWO**
Restates the controlling idea.

■ **STEP THREE**
Offers an opinion, suggestion, summary, or restatement of the topic sentence.

The **conclusion** is the most flexible part of your paragraph. It can be an invitation or a piece of advice to the reader, a restatement of the topic sentence, or a conclusion based on the information in the paragraph. In longer compositions, a conclusion to a paragraph can be both an ending and a beginning. It can introduce the next paragraph in the composition, and, at the same time, it can conclude the paragraph that it is in. However, in this book, you are not learning to write multi-paragraph essays. You are learning to write single paragraphs. The conclusion for this kind of paragraph is not a transition to another main idea; it is the ending of a completely developed idea or opinion.

In the conclusion to a descriptive paragraph, you should do three things:

1. You should repeat or restate the focused topic and give a synonym for the controlling idea, but NOT with exactly the same word that you used in the topic sentence.

Example

John is a very smart person. Bla bla bla bla bla bla bla bla bla. Bla bla bla bla bla; bla, bla bla bla bla bla bla bla bla bla bla bla bla bla bla. Bla bla bla bla bla; bla, bla bla bla bla bla. **As you can see, John is exceptionally intelligent.**

2. You should give an opinion, some advice, or an invitation to the reader or conclude with a general statement about your focused topic.

Example

Howard is an odd little man. Bla bla bla bla bla bla bla bla bla. Bla bla bla bla bla; bla, bla bla bla bla bla bla bla bla bla bla bla bla bla bla. Bla bla bla bla bla; bla, bla bla bla bla bla. **If you come to my town, you should meet this man, and then you will see for yourself why people call him "Weird Howard."**

3. You should relate your conclusion to the support in the paragraph. The conclusion must sound like the logical ending. It finishes developing the controlling idea.

Example

Katherine has beautiful eyes. Bla bla bla bla bla bla bla bla bla. Bla bla bla bla bla; bla, bla bla bla bla bla bla bla bla bla bla bla bla bla bla. Bla bla bla bla bla; bla, bla bla bla bla bla. **People who see Katherine's happy green eyes in the morning feel cheerful the rest of the day.**

Look at the conclusion in the Mona Lisa paragraph below. It gives the writer's opinion of the topic, but it does not use the same words as the topic sentence. It names the topic again and uses a synonym for the controlling idea. You will need to write conclusions like this for your paragraphs of description.

Mona Lisa has the most beautiful eyes in the world. They are large and brown with long lashes, and they have a beautiful almond shape. The expression in her eyes is soft and gentle, and sometimes it seems mystical. When you look into Mona Lisa's eyes, you sense the mystery and honesty of her feelings. **Mona Lisa's eyes are the most expressive eyes that I have ever seen.**

Exercise 3.1 With a partner, write two different concluding sentences for the paragraph above.

1. _____

_____

2. _____

_____

Conclusions should not contradict the controlling idea, give a different controlling idea, or repeat the topic sentence word for word. The conclusion should also name the topic again with a proper noun ("Mary," "Mr. Jones").

Exercise 3.2 What is wrong with the following conclusions to the Mona Lisa paragraph?

1. Mona Lisa's hair also looks very elegant.

_____

2. I don't like Mona Lisa's eyes.

_____

3. Mona has the most beautiful eyes in the world.

_____

4. She has pretty eyes.

_____

Exercise 3.3 Write conclusions for these paragraphs (you saw some of them in the previous chapter). Compare your conclusion with a classmate's conclusions.

When Jennifer is happy, everyone who sees her face feels happy too. She has a wide cheerful smile that delights people. Her impish green eyes light up when she smiles, and they crinkle and shine with happiness. When she is happy, her soft bubbly laughter makes those around her smile. Jennifer always has a sunny expression on her cheerful face....

_____

_____

_____

Henry Jameson has a funny face. His small eyes are crossed, his nose is so tiny that it looks like a button with two holes in it, and his chin is nonexistent. Henry's comical face is covered with a million brown freckles. His thin red hair sticks out all over his head....

_____

_____

_____

My friend Vicky loves to wear eccentric clothing. She wears very long dresses. Over the dress, she wears a short skirt with big holes in it, and sometimes she wears an open blouse over the dress too. Then over all of these clothes, she wears an old vest or sweater. On her head, she wears large floppy hats that have fruit or toy animals on them. On her feet, she wears heavy army boots....

_____

_____

_____

Exercise 3.4 With a classmate, write a paragraph on a separate piece of paper describing an aspect of a famous painting—one that has a person or a face in it if possible. You can use some of the adjectives from the model paragraph, but find others in your dictionary. Make sure your paragraph has a topic sentence, three supporting sentences, and a conclusion. Use concept maps whenever possible, and turn them in with your paragraph.

Exercise 3.5 Write a paragraph on a separate piece of paper about the most **beautiful** person you know. Make a concept map of your ideas before you start your paragraph. Use your dictionary to find adjectives to describe your topic. Before you begin, make a list of all the adjectives you can find that mean the same as "beautiful." Try to use one or two of these adjectives in every sentence in your paragraph.

Examples

pretty	lovely	exotic	gentle	sweet	kind

Exercise 3.6

Part 1 Write a paragraph about yourself. Be sure to indent the first line. Write only five sentences in the paragraph. The first sentence should contain the topic (you) and **one** adjective that will be the controlling idea (*unusual, strange, elegant,* etc.) for your paragraph. Be sure to put a period after each sentence and to begin each new sentence with a capital letter. To help you plan your paragraph, answer the following questions.

1. What three adjectives best describe you? (Examples: *serious, responsible, outgoing, timid, happy, optimistic.*)

   _____   _____   _____

2. Select the one adjective from #1 above that you consider to be your most interesting quality. Write it here:

   _____

3. Think of three ASPECTS that demonstrate that you are _____ . (Write the adjective from #2 in this blank.)

   _____   _____   _____

4. Write several adjectives that describe the three aspects you listed in #3.

_____

_____

_____

Now, using the answer from #2 (above) and your name, write your topic sentence in the middle of this concept map. (Use third person singular for this.) Then put the three aspects from #3 in the attached circles, and use adjectives from #4 for the controlling idea to develop the supporting ideas for the body of the paragraph.

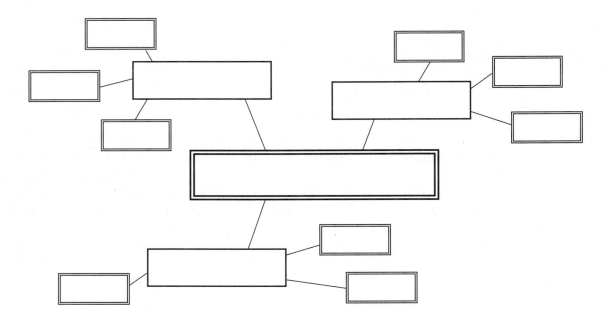

Part 2 Write your paragraph for this concept map. (Don't forget the conclusion!)

_____

_____

_____

_____

_____

_____

Part 3   Exchange paragraphs with a partner. Circle the controlling idea in your partner's paragraph. Underline the focused topic. Count the number of sentences, and put the number at the bottom of your partner's page. Check the conclusion. Does the conclusion rename the focused topic? Does it conclude the paragraph? Write a note to your partner. Tell him/her what you think about the paragraph. Did you like it? Did you learn anything new about your partner?

Part 4   Write three different conclusions for your paragraph about yourself.

1. _____

2. _____

3. _____

JOURNAL ASSIGNMENT

Look at the picture below. Write a paragraph to describe this person's face. You can describe her entire face and use her eyes, mouth, and facial expression as your three aspects, or you can focus on just the expression. Be sure to give her a name and to use that name as the topic in the first sentence. Before you begin your paragraph, plan your controlling idea and support with concept maps, and then make a list of all the adjectives you can find that mean the same as your controlling idea. Use the adjectives in the body of the paragraph. Write a conclusion for your paragraph.

COMPLEX SENTENCES: COORDINATORS, SUBORDINATORS, AND TRANSITIONS

 The computer program that accompanies this section is called: "Connecting Words" (Macintosh and IBM)

Study the concept map and paragraph below.

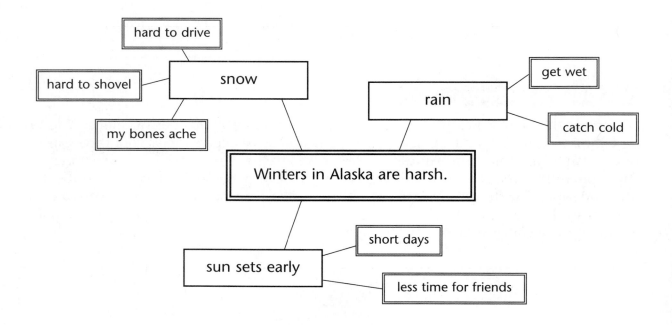

I hate the cold, harsh winters in Alaska. It frequently snows during the winter months, **and because** the cold makes my bones ache, I usually feel miserable for days and days. **In addition,** that heavy snow has to be cleaned off of our sidewalk and driveway almost every week, **and** that gives me sore muscles. **However,** the worst aspect of the Alaskan winters is that the days are very short **because** the sun sets early. This means I have less time to spend with my friends **or** to play sports. Alaska is a beautiful state, **but** I would be much happier if it had shorter and warmer winters!

Look at the paragraph again, and then discuss these questions with a classmate.

1. What kind of support is the writer using?

2. How many supporting sentences are there in the paragraph?

3. What kinds of words are the underlined words in the paragraph, and what do they do for the paragraph?

4. How is the punctuation different for each of the underlined words (look at the commas)?

	Coordinating Conjunctions	Subordinating Conjunctions	Transitional Words and Expressions
Examples	and, but, so, for, yet or, nor	because, if, when, as soon as, before, after, although, while	in addition, also, however, nevertheless afterwards, therefore, consequently
Location	They should NOT begin the first of the combined sentences.	They may begin the first OR the second sentence.	They are always in the second or last sentence.
Use	They can connect complete or incomplete sentences.	They change a complete into an incomplete sentence. Then that incomplete sentence is connected to a complete sentence.	They connect complete sentences.
Punctuation	Put a comma in front of the coordinator to combine complete sentences but NOT if the second sentence is incomplete.	Put a comma in front of a subordinator if you begin your sentence with the dependent clause but NOT if you begin with the independent clause.	Almost always use a comma after a transition. You may use a semicolon or a period in front of the transition word. Use commas around transition words when they are inside the sentence.

Subordinators

As you can see from the chart above, subordinating conjunctions are different from coordinating conjunctions.

1. Coordinating conjunctions should NOT begin a sentence. They only connect one sentence to another, and they are put in front of the second sentence (not the first).

   Example

   John is going to the beach, **and** his brother is going with him.

   Subordinating conjunctions are more flexible and can be put at the beginning of the first or second sentence.

   Examples

   John is going to the beach **because** the sun is shining.

   Because the sun is shining, John is going to the beach.

2. Coordinating conjunctions can connect complete sentences (making compound sentences), and each sentence expresses a complete idea. Subordinating conjunctions change a complete sentence into a dependent clause (not a complete idea). Then that sentence needs to be connected to an **independent clause** (a complete sentence).

3. The punctuation is different for coordinators and subordinators.

● Punctuation Rules for Subordinators

To write a sentence with a subordinating conjunction, you need to remember two rules for punctuation:

1. If you begin your sentence with the subordinate clause (the sentence that begins with the subordinator), put a comma after the clause.

   Example

   complete sentence: Sharon felt ill.

   complete sentence: Sharon went home early yesterday.

   subordinator: because

   subordinate clause: Because Sharon felt ill

   complete sentence: Because Sharon felt ill, she went home early yesterday.

   ↑
   COMMA

2. If you begin your sentence with the independent clause, you usually do not need a comma after the independent clause.

Example

INDEPENDENT CLAUSE   SUBORDINATE CLAUSE

Professor Garcia will be surprised   if Jaime comes to class early every day.

↑

NO COMMA GOES HERE

Exercise 3.7   Add commas wherever necessary.

1. When I watch television ___ I like to eat popcorn.

2. I like to eat popcorn ___ when I watch television.

3. We will begin to study Chapter 3 ___ after we finish Chapter 2.

4. After we finish Chapter 2 ___ we will begin to study Chapter 3.

5. Because I believed him ___ I left the class early.

6. I left the class early ___ because I believed him.

7. I am going to get wet ___ because it is raining.

8. Because it is raining ___ I am going to get wet.

9. Margarita speaks Portuguese ___ because she is from Brazil.

10. Because Margarita is from Brazil ___ she speaks Portuguese.

Exercise 3.8   Change the position of the subordinate clause. If it is first, put it last. If it is last, put it first. Make all the necessary changes with punctuation.

Examples

Maritza was late to class today because her car had a flat tire.

     Because Maritza's car had a flat tire, she was late to class today.

  or   Because her car had a flat tire, Maritza was late to class today.

Ana Maria loves her living room because it is beautiful and comfortable.

     Because her living room is beautiful and comfortable, Ana Maria loves it.

  or   Because Ana Maria's living room is beautiful and comfortable, she loves it.

1. Because we have a test tomorrow, we need to go to the library.

   _____

2. Oneida is absent because she is sick.

   _____

3. Adriana likes that restaurant because it has good pasta.

   _____

4. Because the weather was nice, we stayed in the park.

   _____

5. Francia helps her friends because she is a generous person.

   _____

6. Maria awoke early because she felt bad.

   _____

• The Logic of the Subordinating Conjunction *because*

You show the logic of your sentence with the subordinator you use. Look at the difference in meaning in these examples:

correct: Because President Lincoln believed in civil rights, he was against slavery.

wrong: Because Lincoln was president, he was assassinated. **(not logical)**

When you use *because,* your sentence must show a cause (or reason) and an effect (or result). Write the CAUSE after the word *because.* Write the result or effect in the other part of the sentence. Look at the example above again. Can you tell why it is not logical?[1]

Example

correct: Because it is raining outside, we are going to get wet.

wrong: It is raining outside because we are going to get wet.

The second example is wrong because it means that the reason for the rain is that we will get wet. It is illogical. The sentence confuses the cause with the effect.

---

1 It is illogical because the statement implies that ALL presidents are assassinated and that the only reason for Lincoln's assassination was that he was a president.

Exercise 3.9 Logical or illogical? Write "L" in front of the logical sentences and "I" in front of the illogical sentences.

L / I

___ 1. I will marry you because I love your personality.

___ 2. Because I will marry you, I love your personality.

___ 3. Because the baby is sleeping, you must be quiet.

___ 4. The baby is sleeping because you must be quiet.

Exercise 3.10 Do this exercise with a classmate. Use the following concept map and the model paragraph at the beginning of this section to write a paragraph. Try to use the word *because* two times in your paragraph. You do not need to use all of the details in the concept map, and you may change any of the ideas or add your own. (Don't forget your conclusion!)

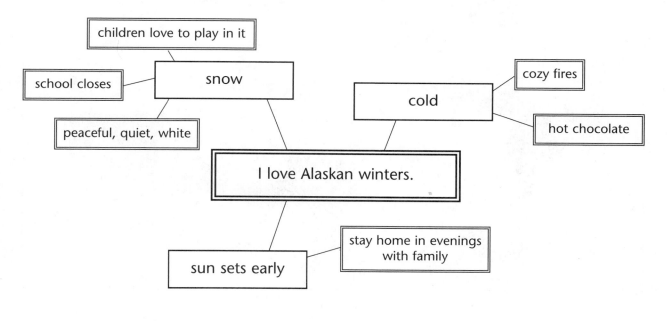

_____

_____

_____

_____

_____

_____

Exercise 3.11 With a classmate, describe the following pictures orally, and then write two or three sentences about each one. Use *because* in your sentences.

- ***If*: Subordinator of Condition (No Future Tense Possible); Subordinator of Willingness, Refusal, or Request (Future Tense Possible)**

    If you live in Hawaii or Florida, you should prepare for hurricanes.

    If you exercise every day, you will stay in good shape.

You can use *if* to show a condition. The information in the independent clause must be the logical result or consequence of that condition. You do not use the future tense with *if* clauses if the meaning is conditional. However, you can use *will* with *if* to make a request or to show willingness or refusal to do something.

Examples of *if* for willingness or refusal:

If you will (please) come early tomorrow [,] we can finish the project quickly.
          WILLINGNESS   CONSEQUENCE

If the baby won't eat his food [,] try to give him a bottle of milk. (= if the baby refuses)
          REFUSAL   CONSEQUENCE

Examples of *if* for conditions:

If you drive too fast [,] you can get a speeding ticket.
          CONDITION   CONSEQUENCE

You should go to the doctor **if** you have a high fever.
          CONSEQUENCE   CONDITION

Exercise 3.12 Interview a partner in class and finish these sentences with the information you get from your partner. (Remember: Don't use the future tense after *if!!*)

1. My partner will be happy if _____ .

2. My partner will be very sad if _____ .

3. If this class has an exam today, my partner _____ .

Circle the ERROR in each of the following sentences, and then rewrite the sentence correctly.

1. If it won't rain tomorrow, we will hold class outside in the patio area.

   _____

2. We cannot have class outside if it will rain.

   _____

3. If you will want to go with me to the beach, I'll pick you up at 9:30.

   _____

4. I will never finish this book if you will not stop disturbing me!

   _____

Exercise 3.13 Do this exercise with a partner. Use coordinating conjunctions *(and, but,* and *so)* or subordinators *(because* and *if)* to combine these sentences. There will be more than one possible answer for most of these exercises.

1. The economy of that country is deteriorating more each day. / The leader will probably fall this year.

   _____

   _____

2. The movie *Gone with the Wind* was dramatic. / I enjoyed it very much. / I recommend it to you.

   _____

   _____

3. Henry asked Maria to have lunch with him. / Maria agreed. / She was hungry, too. / They had to hurry. / They only had 30 minutes to eat.

   _____

   _____

4. This exercise is not difficult. / The students are having trouble with it. / The vocabulary in the exercise must be difficult.

   _____

   _____

5. (if) It might rain. / We should take an umbrella.

   _____

   _____

Transitional Words and Expressions

The computer program that accompanies this section is called: "Connecting Words" (Macintosh and IBM)

A third group of connecting words are **transitional words** (conjunctive adverbs) and **transitional expressions.** They show relationships between ideas. They connect one complete sentence to another complete sentence or one paragraph to another paragraph. In paragraphs, they show the transition (change) from one supporting idea to the next supporting idea, and they show the logical relation between those ideas.

• Punctuation Rules for Transitions

There are three common patterns of punctuation for transitional words.

Pattern #1

Complete sentence　　;　　transitional word　　,　　complete sentence.

Pattern #2

Complete sentence　　.　　Transitional word　　,　　complete sentence.

Pattern #3

Complete sentence　　.　　Subject　　,　　trans. word　　,　　verb

Complete sentence　　.　　Subject + auxiliary　　,　　trans. word　　,　　main verb…

Examples

Pattern #1

I have to get up early ⟨ ; ⟩ ⟨ h ⟩owever ⟨ , ⟩ I don't have an alarm clock.

Pattern #2

I have to get up early ⟨ . ⟩ ⟨ H ⟩owever ⟨ , ⟩ I don't have an alarm clock.

Pattern #3

John has an alarm clock ⟨ . ⟩ I ⟨ , ⟩ however ⟨ , ⟩ ⟨ do ⟩ not have one, so I wake up late.

I don't have an alarm clock ⟨ . ⟩ I ⟨ do, ⟩ however ⟨ , ⟩ have a wall clock.

• *However, nevertheless*

There are lots of people there. **However,** I do not recognize any of them.

The words *however* and *nevertheless* mean the same as *but.* They show contrast or surprise, and they mean "on the contrary" or "differently." When you use *however* or *nevertheless,* the information in the second sentence contrasts with the information in the first.

Examples

The walls in this room are dark; **however,** the carpet is light.

The chalkboard is clean. **However,** the erasers are full of chalk.

This room is big; **nevertheless,** it feels small because it is so crowded.

The television in the corner is new. **Nevertheless,** it doesn't work well.

Exercise 3.14 Use correct punctuation and capital letters where necessary, and fill in the blanks with *however, nevertheless, because,* or *but.*

1. The living room is cool; _____ , the dining room is hot.

2. The living room is cool, _____ the kitchen is hot.

3. _____ the dining room is hot, we will eat in the living room today.

4. There are many desks in the middle of the room, _____ there are very few desks in the back of the room.

5. The desks in the back of the room are empty _____ most of the students are absent today.

6. There are many desks in the front of the room; _____ , there are very few desks in the back of the room.

7. The teacher's desk is messy. Her table, _____ , is neat.

8. The teacher's desk is messy, _____ her table is neat.

9. The red car is expensive. _____ , the green one is cheap.

10. The red car is expensive, _____ the green one is cheap.

● *In addition, also*

There are lots of students in the auditorium. There are **also** lots of teachers there.

There are lots of students in the auditorium. **In addition,** there are lots of teachers there.

The words *in addition* and *also* are used to show additional information. *In addition* is punctuated like other transition words, but *also* is different. When *also* is written inside the sentence, it doesn't need commas around it.

Examples

The walls in this room are dark; **in addition,** the carpet and ceiling are dark.

The chalkboard is clean. **In addition,** the carpet and ceiling are clean.

The chalkboard is clean. The carpet and ceiling, **in addition,** are clean.

This room is dark; **also,** the carpet and ceiling are dark.

John usually enjoys going to the movies with his friends. **Also,** he likes to go to dinner with them.

The exception

The television in the corner is new. The carpet and ceiling are **also** new. **(no commas)**

John usually enjoys going to the movies with his friends on Saturdays. He **also** likes to go to dinner with them.

Exercise 3.15 Use correct punctuation and capital letters where necessary, and fill in the blanks with *also, in addition,* or *and.*

1. The living room is cool; _____ , the dining room is cool, too.

2. The living room is cool, _____ the dining room is cool, too.

3. The living room is cool. The dining room is _____ cool.

4. There are many desks in the middle of the room, _____ there are _____ many desks in the back of the room.

5. The living room is cool. _____ , the dining room is cool, too.

Exercise 3.16 Combine these sentences using *in addition* and *also.* When the transition word is written with a capital letter, end the preceding sentence with a period.

Example

John cooked dinner. He washed the dishes. He cleaned the kitchen.

John cooked dinner. **In addition,** he washed the dishes and cleaned the kitchen.

John cooked dinner; **in addition,** he washed the dishes and cleaned the kitchen.

John cooked dinner. **He also** washed the dishes and cleaned the kitchen.

John cooked dinner. **Also,** he washed the dishes and cleaned the kitchen.

John cooked dinner; **also,** he washed the dishes and cleaned the kitchen.

1. When you wash the dishes, you need to use soap to get all of the food off them. / You need to rinse all of the soap off the dishes before you dry them.

(in addition) _____

(In addition) _____

(also) _____

(Also) _____

(also) _____

2. Rosemary plays volleyball. / She is a member of the school tennis team.

(In addition) _____

(in addition) _____

(also) _____

(Also) _____

(also) _____

3. Patricia and Ariel study computer programming. / They take courses in chemistry and history.

(In addition) _____

(in addition) _____

(Also) _____

(also) _____

(also) _____

• *Afterwards* (Transition Word) and *after* (Subordinator)

John invited Marie to dinner to celebrate their anniversary. They had a lovely dinner. **Afterwards,** he realized that he didn't have enough money to pay the bill. He was embarrassed. **After** he apologized to Marie, he asked her to lend him money to pay the bill.

Afterwards is a transition word, and it means "then" or "after that." It is frequently confused with *after,* but be careful! The two words mean just the opposite of each other. *After* is a subordinator (punctuated like *because).*

Examples

        FIRST ACTION   SECOND ACTION
First we bought the tickets. **Afterwards,** we went into the theater.

We bought the tickets **after** we went into the theater.
    SECOND ACTION   FIRST ACTION

In the first sentence, we bought the tickets outside the theater and then went in. In the second sentence, we went into the theater first and bought the tickets inside. You can see that *afterwards* means the opposite of *after.*

You try it: Combine these sentences. Keep the same order and use correct punctuation. Write each sentence three different ways.

1. First we went to the store. Then we went to school.

   _____ afterwards _____

   _____ after _____

   After _____   _____

2. First he goes to the library. Then he goes to class.

   _____ Afterwards _____

   _____ after _____

   After _____   _____

3. First he misses class. Then he calls the teacher.

   _____ afterwards _____

   _____ after _____

   After _____   _____

4. First it rains. Then it snows.

   _____ Afterwards _____

   _____ after _____

   After _____   _____

● *Therefore* and *consequently*

The music was too loud. **Therefore,** I got a headache.

The music was too loud; **consequently,** I got a headache.

Therefore and *consequently* show a result. The sentence after *therefore* or *consequently* must show the result or consequence of the sentence that precedes those words.

The students didn't study last week. Therefore, they failed the test yesterday.

CAUSE   EFFECT

The students didn't study last week. Consequently, they failed the test yesterday.

CAUSE   EFFECT

Exercise 3.17 Write complete sentences using these words. You may change the order of these words, add words, and/or make some verbs negative to make the sentences complete and logical. If the word in parentheses has a capital letter, write it first in the sentence or (for transition words) after a period.

1.
    a. (so) / weather / bad / stay indoors (imperative)

    _____

    b. (Because) / weather / good / you / stay indoors

    _____

    c. (because) / weather / bad / they / go to the park

    _____

    d. (consequently) / weather / bad / she / stay indoors

    _____

    e. (Consequently) / weather / good / I / stay indoors

    _____

2.
    a. (so) / students / intelligent / pass the class

    _____

    b. (because) / students / intelligent / pass the class

    _____

    c. (Because) / students / intelligent / pass the class

    _____

    d. (therefore) / students / intelligent / pass the class

    _____

    e. (Therefore) students / intelligent / pass the class

    _____

3.
    a. (so) / economy / bad / people / worry

    _____

b. (Because) / cake / delicious / Jane / eat three slices

_____

c. (because) / weather / bad / people / carry umbrellas

_____

d. (therefore) / explanation / bad / students / understand

_____

e. (Therefore) / music / loud / Tom / get headache

_____

4.
   a. (so) / Jan / home / daughter / ill / yesterday

_____

   b. (because) / Iris / be / late / car / break down

_____

   c. (Because) / Louis / call a friend / need / math assignment

_____

   d. (Consequently) Jenny / win / dance contest / receive / trophy

_____

5.
   a. (so) / Sharon / win / scholarship / study / Harvard

_____

   b. (because) / Beatriz / buy / car / drive / school

_____

   c. (Because) / television / work / Chris / listen / music

_____

   d. (therefore) / television / break / Elio / watch / favorite program

_____

   e. (Therefore) / Susan / late to work / boss / be angry

_____

WRITING ASSIGNMENTS

Find three paragraphs that you wrote as assignments for previous chapters. For each of the assignments, write two different conclusions.

Rewrite one of your paragraphs using the sentence connectors you learned in this chapter. Try to add more details to your paragraph.

VOCABULARY BUILDING

Write eight new vocabulary words that you learned in class this week. Next to each word, write a synonym for the word (or the translation of the word in your own language if you cannot find a synonym). Then write the word in a sentence.

1. _____

_____

2. _____

_____

3. _____

_____

4. _____

_____

5. _____

_____

6. _____

_____

7. _____

_____

8. _____

_____

FOR THE TEACHER'S INFORMATION

Write for ten minutes. The topic is "This writing class and me." You can write anything you want about your experience in this class: what you are learning, what you would like to learn, what you like, what you do not like, how the class could be better, and so on.

chapter
four

Describing Personality Traits

■ **STEP ONE**
Select the aspects that prove the controlling idea.

■ **STEP TWO**
Select actions for the aspects.

■ **STEP THREE**
Add adverbs of frequency.

There are many different aspects of a person, place, or object that you can describe. For example, when you describe people, you can describe their size, shape, attitude, personality, habits, features (face, teeth, smile), intelligence, and so on. The possibilities are almost endless. As you write your description, you use adjectives to add details to your three supporting sentences, but if you want to describe someone's *personality traits,* you often need to describe behaviors and actions. Adverbs and frequency adverbs can help you do this. Adverbs of frequency can also add a dramatic tone to the actions you are describing.

Look at the following examples. The adverb in the second of each pair of sentences changes the image produced by the sentence.

Mary bites her nails.

Mary **always** bites her nails. **(more dramatic)**

Mary is biting her nails.

Mary is **always** biting her nails. **(This bothers you.)**

John doesn't get angry.

John **never** gets angry. **(more dramatic)**

Look at the concept map used to plan the model paragraph. Then, use words from the list to fill in the blanks with the missing adverbs of frequency.

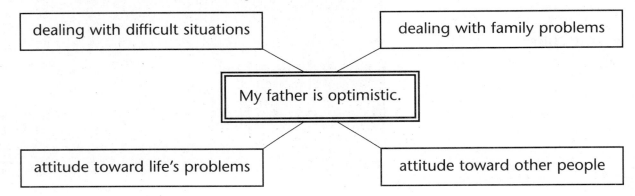

dealing with difficult situations		dealing with family problems
	My father is optimistic.	
attitude toward life's problems		attitude toward other people

**always   usually   seldom   almost never
sometimes   rarely   never   almost always
frequently   often   generally**

One of my father's best qualities is his marvelous optimism. He is _____ sad or

depressed and is _____ able to see the bright side of even the most difficult situa-

tion. With his sense of humor, he _____ makes our family's problems seem trivial.

He _____ tells me that there is good in everybody and a reason for everything that happens. In fact, he believes that even life's most unpleasant experiences can _____ be good for us if we learn something positive from them. I love my father's optimism and his joy for life.

Exercise 4.1 With a classmate for a partner, discuss these questions about this paragraph:

1. Read the paragraph to a classmate without the adverbs of frequency. Then read the paragraph again with the adverbs. How do the adverbs of frequency change the tone of the paragraph?

2. Look at the paragraph again, and fill in the concept map below with the controlling idea for each of the three aspects that is developed in the paragraph. The first one is done for you.

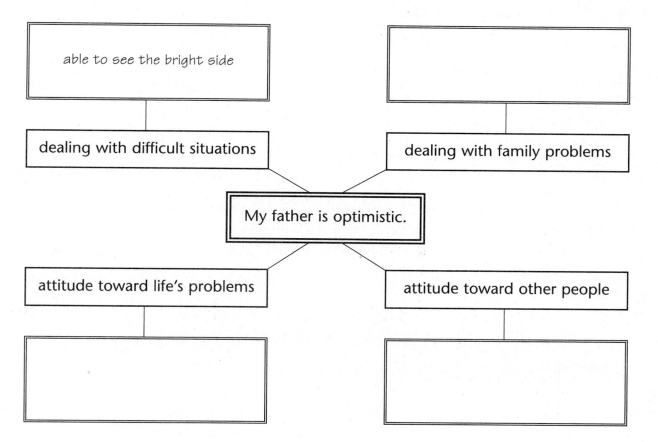

Exercise 4.2   Write a paragraph about your favorite (or least favorite) friend using the paragraph above as a model. Exchange paragraphs with a classmate, and check for the following details:

1. How many periods are in your partner's paragraph? _____ (There should be five to eight.)

2. Circle the verbs in the paragraph. (Do they agree with the subject? Do the verbs that are about "he" or "she" in the present tense end with -*s*?)

3. Underline the focused topic and the controlling idea in the topic sentence.

4. Is there a conclusion to the paragraph? Do you like the conclusion?

Return papers and discuss your answers with your partner.

ADVERBS OF FREQUENCY

The computer program that accompanies this section is called: "Adverbs of Frequency" (Macintosh and IBM)

You can see from the model paragraph that adverbs of frequency give a general idea of **how often** you repeat an action or activity. In the next section of this chapter, you will study what frequency adverbs mean and how and where they are used in sentences.

When someone asks, "Do you ever go to the beach?," you can answer with an adverb of frequency: "Yes, I **sometimes** do." If people want a more specific idea of frequency, they will ask, "How often do you go to the beach?" In this case you should use a more specific expression of frequency such as: "I **(usually)** go to the beach about **once a month.**"

Other time expressions include:

once in a while	from time to time	(every) now and then	every two weeks
once a week	all the time	every other day	on the weekends

Time expressions that are not adverbs of frequency usually go at the beginning of a sentence followed by a comma or after the verb and objects.

Examples

Once in a while, I like to read mystery books.

Most of the time, I prefer to read science fiction novels or biographies.

We usually go to the beach with our friends **on the weekends.**

I go out with my cousins **from time to time.**

100% of the time	= *always*
85% of the time	= *usually, generally*
45% of the time	= *frequently, often*
30% of the time	= *sometimes, occasionally*
10% of the time	= *seldom*
5% of the time	= *rarely*
0% of the time	= *never*

Position of Adverbs of Frequency

When you use adverbs of frequency, put them in the following positions in sentences.

Affirmative	→	I am **usually** here.
		We **often** stay late.
Negative	→	I don't **always** understand.
		She won't **ever** forget it.
Questions	→	Do you **always** go?
		Is she **sometimes** loud?
Short Answers	→	Yes, they **frequently** do.
		No, I **never** am.
Exceptions	→	**Usually** I am early to class.
		I am **usually** early to class.
		I am early to class **usually.**

● In Affirmative Sentences

Put frequency adverbs before the main verb in a sentence, EXCEPT for the verb "be." Adverbs go after the verb "be" in affirmative sentences.

Examples

I *am* **always** happy on Fridays.

I **usually** *put* the flowers on the shelf.

She **never** *sings* the right notes.

John *is* **seldom** sad.

• In Negative Sentences

Put frequency adverbs after the auxiliary verb in negative sentences.

Examples

I don't **always** finish my homework.

Jaime can't **always** remember the spelling rules.

She doesn't **ever** come late to class.

I will **never** lose my keys.

• In Questions

In questions, put the adverb of frequency after the subject.

Examples

Does Francia **always** cook a big breakfast in the morning?

Is this class **ever** boring? (Of course it isn't!!!)

Exercise 4.3   Write sentences using the following groups of words.

1. you / always / do / homework / this class

   _____

2. you / usually / listen to music / English

   _____

3. you / sometimes / arrive / late to class

   _____

4. you / rarely / be / early to class

   _____

Now change the same sentences into questions.

1. you / always / do / homework / this class?

   _____

2. you / ever / listen to music / English?

   _____

3. you / sometimes / arrive / late to class?

_____

4. you / sometimes / be / early to class?

_____

Ask classmates the questions you have just written, and write their responses here. Be sure to include an adverb of frequency in each sentence.

1. _____

2. _____

3. _____

4. _____

In Short Answers

In a short answer, put the frequency adverb between the subject and the verb for ALL verbs.

Examples

Do you ever use a red pen? No, I **never** do. Yes, I **often** do.

Are you ever tired in the morning? No, I **never** am. Yes, I **sometimes** am.

Exercise 4.4 With a classmate, write these answers as short answers.

Example

Yes, I often use a red pen. = Yes, I often do.

Yes, I am often early to class. = Yes, I often am.

1. Yes, I often study hard on the weekends. _____

2. Yes, I am always hungry in the afternoon. _____

3. No, I never go to the beach during the week. _____

• "Flexible" Adverbs of Frequency

Often, sometimes, and *usually* are more flexible. You can also put them at the beginning (and sometimes at the end) of a sentence.

Examples

Sometimes it rains in the summer months in Miami.

We **usually** do not have writing class early in the morning.

María goes to the lab to do her exercises **often.**

Exercise 4.5 Write things you usually do on the weekends.

1. _____

2. _____

3. _____

Write three questions for a classmate using "Do you ever…?"

1. _____

2. _____

3. _____

Ask your classmate these questions and write his/her responses. Use adverbs of frequency or time expressions in your sentences.

1. _____

2. _____

3. _____

Use of Adverbs of Frequency in Affirmative, Negative, and Interrogative Sentences

Frequency adverbs for affirmative statements are:

always	I **always** do my homework. She **always** works late on Mondays.

usually / generally	Jaime **usually** studies at night. He is **generally** a good student.
often / frequently	We **often** cannot go to bed early. The back door is **frequently** locked.
sometimes / occasionally	You **sometimes** forget to call. He is **occasionally** late.

When you use a negative adverb of frequency in a sentence, you do not need to make your verb negative. The adverb makes the sentence negative. The frequency adverbs for negative statements are:

| *seldom / rarely / hardly ever* | Lissett **hardly ever** speaks in class. She **seldom** speaks. |
| *almost never / never* | You **never** come to my house. You **almost never** call me. |

Exercise 4.6 Sit with a classmate. Write five sentences about what your partner *rarely, seldom, never, almost never,* or *hardly ever* does on Sundays.

1. _____
2. _____
3. _____
4. _____
5. _____

Use of *ever*

Ever can be used with a **negative** verb and in **questions (affirmative or negative)** when you want an answer that tells frequency. When *ever* is used with a negative verb, it means the same as "never."

Examples

Oneida doesn't **ever** go to work on Sundays. = Oneida **never** goes to work on Sundays.

Judith shouldn't **ever** wear red. = Judith should **never** wear red.

Do you **ever** study on Friday nights? Yes, I often do.

Are**n't** you **ever** tired of studying? Yes, I sometimes am.

Exercise 4.7 Write sentences using adverbs of frequency. Remember to use *ever* in the questions.

I / drink / coffee / morning
I usually drink coffee in the morning.

1. we / be / late to class

   _____

2. Sharon / study / on / Saturday night

   _____

3. your / father / come to visit you?

   _____

4. you / be / absent / from class?

   _____

5. you / have / a headache / in the afternoon?

   _____

6. your sister / be / sick?

   _____

7. these lessons / be / hard

   _____

8. the students / ask / questions

   _____

9. It / be / hot / in Toronto

   _____

10. tornadoes / be / dangerous

   _____

Exercise 4.8 Write questions using the following groups of words. You may add any words you want. Use *ever* in your questions.

Examples

take / bath / night
Do you ever take a bath at night?

be / sleepy / afternoon
Are you ever sleepy in the afternoon?

1. cook / Sunday afternoons

_____

2. be / tired / morning

_____

3. smoke

_____

4. be / grouchy / friends

_____

5. go out on the weekends

_____

Exercise 4.9 Now use the questions you have just written to interview a classmate. Your classmate will interview you too. When your partner answers "yes" to any question, continue asking questions about that topic and find out more. Write his/her responses below. Tell your partner to use adverbs of frequency.

Example

Your conversation:
You: Do you **ever** travel to foreign countries?
Kim: Yes, I **sometimes** do. What about you?
You: I do too. Tell me about your travels. Where do you **usually** go?
Kim: (answer…) and then, "What about you?"
You: (answer…)

You write:

Kim sometimes travels to foreign countries. He often goes to Mexico during Christmas vacation.

1. _____

2. _____

3. _____

4. _____

5. _____

Exercise 4.10   Add adverbs of frequency to this paragraph to give it an interesting tone. Space is left on both sides of the words. Add an adverb in the correct location. You must decide which side is correct.

John is the rudest person in our class. He (1) _____ interrupts _____ other students when they are speaking and (2) _____ tries _____ to answer every question for them; in fact, (3) _____ , he even interrupts the teacher while she is trying to explain a point to the class. When this happens, he (4) _____ raises _____ his hand but just breaks in and shouts his question in a loud voice. In addition, John (5) _____ comes _____ late to class, and he (6) _____ enters _____ the room quietly. On the contrary, he (7) _____ greets _____ the class loudly, even if the teacher is in the middle of an exercise, and that's not all. He (8) _____ walks _____ out of class two or three times during class without asking permission. This person (9) _____ exhibits _____ such rude behavior that I think the teacher should expel him from our class.

Using Adverbs of Frequency to Add Tone to Paragraphs

The following series of concept maps were used to plan two paragraphs. The topic for both paragraphs was "friends." Notice that the writer first used a concept map to focus the topic, listing the names of five good friends:

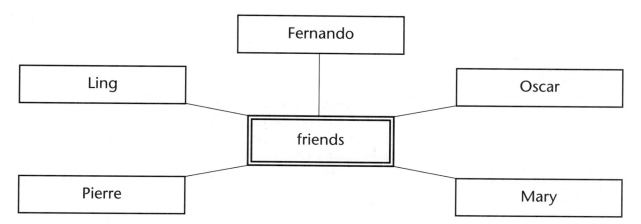

Next the writer had to select one of these focused topics for the paragraph:

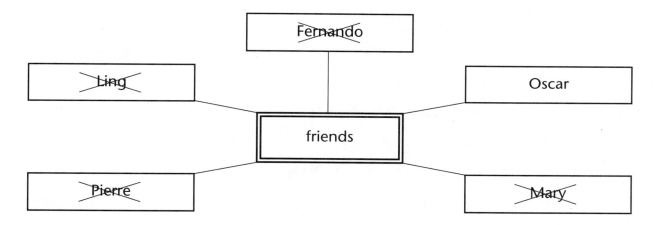

After the topic had a focus, the next step was to find a controlling idea for the paragraph about Oscar:

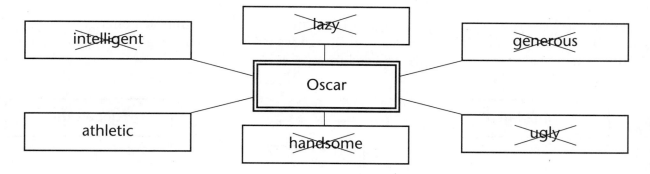

The controlling idea "athletic" was selected, and the writer then brainstormed and created a concept map for the supporting ideas of the paragraph.

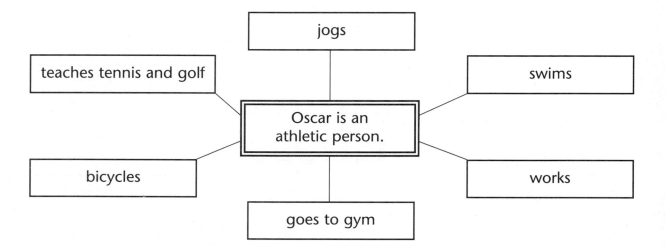

The writer then added adverbs of frequency and time expressions such as "every day" and "on the weekends" to the details of the paragraph. This created a special "tone" to the description. In this paragraph, fill in the blanks with adverbs of frequency and time expressions.

Oscar is a very athletic person. (1) _____ _____ , before he goes to his

job, where he teaches tennis and golf, he (2) _____ _____ jogs five miles

and swims thirty laps in the pool. He (3) _____ works at least eight hours and

(4) _____ as many as twelve, and after work, he (5) _____ goes to the gym

to work out on the machines. (6) _____ _____ _____ , Oscar takes

long bicycle rides in the country or enters marathons or races. In fact, Oscar is such an

active person that you will (7) _____ see him just sitting down and relaxing.

Notice how the same focused topic with a different controlling idea changes the paragraph. In the paragraph below, the controlling idea is "lazy." Notice, also, how the adverbs of frequency give the paragraph a special tone.

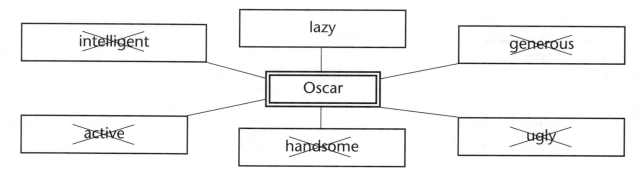

Here is the concept map for the support in the paragraph you see below.

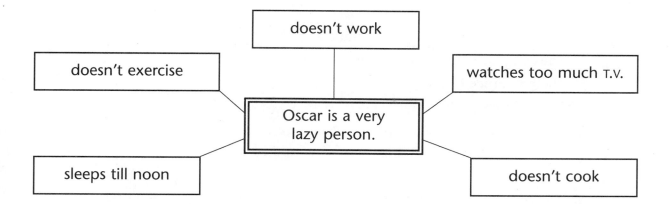

Oscar is a very LAZY person.   He nearly always sleeps until noon, and he never looks for a job. He almost always spends his day at home on the couch watching television for eight or nine hours, or reading magazines and newspapers, and he rarely exercises. He seldom even prepares his own food. He asks his mother or brother to prepare his lunch before they go to work, and he is so lazy that he generally asks them to leave the food on the table near his chair because he doesn't want to walk to the kitchen. If Oscar continues with this inactive, overindulgent lifestyle, I think he will have a heart attack.

Exercise 4.11 Circle the adverbs of frequency and time expressions in the above paragraph.

THE BODY AND CONCLUSION OF THE PARAGRAPH (ACTIONS AND PERSONALITY TRAITS)

Exercise 4.12 Look at the topic sentence in the box, and identify which sentences would develop the controlling idea of that topic sentence. Write "Y" in the blank to the left of the sentence if the sentence would develop the controlling idea in the topic sentence. Write "N" if the sentence would NOT develop the controlling idea.

Romelia Yobst is the most talented artist in Eureka.

Y / N

___ 1. Her paintings are becoming valuable.

___ 2. She can paint almost anything she sees.

___ 3. She has a nice house.

___ 4. She is a nice person.

___ 5. She teaches painting at three universities.

___ 6. Her cheerful, colorful art expresses her optimism.

___ 7. She likes my son.

___ 8. The portrait that she painted of my son is now worth a lot of money.

___ 9. I bought a car from her last year.

___ 10. She is becoming famous.

Lee Danner is the most versatile person I know.

Y / N

___ 1. He can build a house by himself.

___ 2. He can repair almost any electrical or plumbing problem.

___ 3. He can repair autos and trucks.

___ 4. He is a talented painter and a sculptor.

___ 5. He has red hair.

___ 6. He is married to my sister.

___ 7. He is a surveyor.

___ 8. He is a commercial fisherman.

___ 9. He is a landscaper.

___ 10. He is a nice person.

Everyone who knows Dorothy Gardner admires her for her generosity.

Y / N

___ 1. She volunteers her time at the local hospital each week.

___ 2. She loves to eat in fancy restaurants.

___ 3. She helps her friends, family, and neighbors with their personal problems.

___ 4. She works at Safeway.

___ 5. She donates money to charity each year.

___ 6. She stops to help strangers who are stranded on the road.

___ 7. She has blue eyes.

___ 8. She lends her new car to friends when they need it.

___ 9. She likes to travel.

___ 10. She collects clothes and food for the homeless.

These paragraphs use the sentences from the previous exercise. Each paragraph needs a conclusion. You may write a whole paragraph with your partner for the last group of sentences about Dorothy Gardner.

Romelia Yobst is probably the most talented artist in Eureka. She can paint almost anything she sees, and her cheerful, colorful art expresses her optimism. Her paintings are becoming valuable. In fact, the portrait she painted of my son a few years ago is now worth a lot of money. Romelia is becoming famous. She now teaches painting at three universities....

_____

_____

Lee Danner is the most versatile person I know. He earns his living as a surveyor and commercial fisherman, but his talents do not end there. He is a talented carpenter and handyman, and he can build a house by himself and repair almost any electrical or mechanical problem that comes up. In addition, he is a talented artist and sculptor and frequently exhibits his work in Mendocino galleries....

_____

_____

Write the paragraph about Dorothy Gardner here:

_____

_____

_____

_____

_____

Exercise 4.13 Do this exercise with a partner. Finish these three concept maps with details about the person's activities and then select ONE of the three maps from which to write a paragraph.

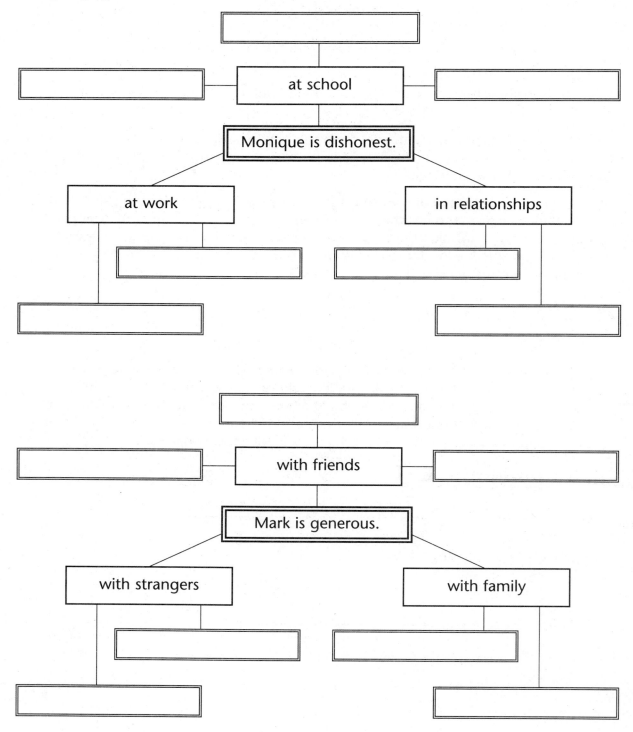

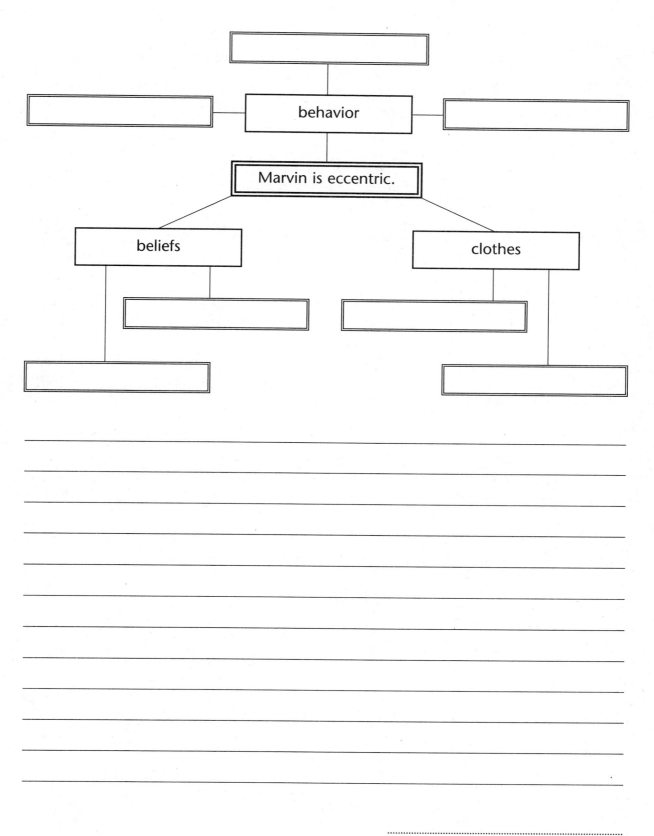

| behavior |

| Marvin is eccentric. |

| beliefs | | clothes |

_____

_____

_____

_____

_____

_____

_____

_____

_____

_____

_____

_____

Exercise 4.14 Fill in the following concept map with the name of your best friend and several adjectives that describe his or her activities (examples: *responsible, busy, thoughtful, nervous).*

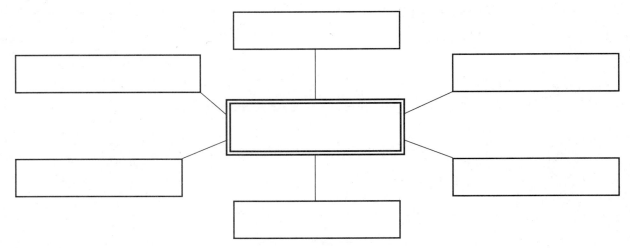

Now select ONE of the adjectives and brainstorm for supporting details that demonstrate the adjective. Do not use "nice" or "good." Write a paragraph using this support, and add adverbs of frequency to give your paragraph tone.

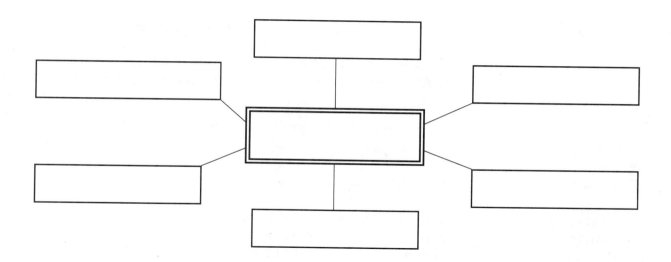

Exercise 4.15 Journal assignment: Write a paragraph describing your favorite teacher. After you decide on your controlling idea, describe the actions (using adverbs of frequency wherever possible) that demonstrate the controlling idea.

Example

Roy Schual is my favorite teacher because he is such a fair person. He always makes everyone in his class feel important and …

PRONOUNS AND POSSESSIVE ADJECTIVES

The computer programs that accompany this section are called: "Building Sentences" (Macintosh) and "Pronouns and Possessive Adjectives" (IBM)

Using pronouns and possessive adjectives helps you avoid sounding repetitive, and using demonstrative adjectives (*this, that, these,* and *those*) makes any *necessary* repetitions sound fluent. Read the following paragraph, and notice how strange the repetition of the same noun forms sounds.

Julio Iglesias is one of the most popular singers in the world today. **Julio Iglesias** is popular with people from around the world. First of all, **Julio Iglesias** sings songs in many different languages, which means that people from many different countries can enjoy **Julio Iglesias'** wonderful romantic voice. Another reason for **Julio Iglesias'** popularity is the fact that **Julio Iglesias** appeals to women of all ages. **Julio Iglesias** has a face that is neither young nor old, so most women find **Julio Iglesias** attractive. Also, **Julio Iglesias'** songs contribute to his popularity. **Julio**

Iglesias prefers to sing romantic songs that appeal to the heart and soul, as well as famous traditional songs from different countries that are already familiar and well-loved. Most people are in the mood to hear **Julio Iglesias'** style of song at least once in a while. In my opinion, **Julio Iglesias** is the most romantic Spanish singer that has ever lived.

You can see from the above paragraph how important pronouns are. The paragraph sounds absurd. Let's learn how to use pronouns correctly, and then we can correct this paragraph.

Look at the following chart of pronouns and possessive adjectives.

Subject Pronouns	Object Pronouns	Possessive Adjectives (Followed by Noun)	Possessive Pronouns (Not Followed by Noun)
I	me	my	mine
you	you	your	yours
he	him	his	his
she	her	her	hers
it	it	its	
we	us	our	ours
you	you	your	yours
they	them	their	theirs

Demonstrative Pronouns
(Noun Optional)

this	these
that	those

How to Use Pronouns and Possessive Adjectives

Subject pronouns replace proper nouns (names of people or things, for example). They go before (in front of) the main verb in a sentence.

Examples

I am here.	= **I** am here.
Mary is my sister.	= **She** is my sister.
Mark went home	= **He** went home.
Steve and John study here.	= **They** study here.

Object pronouns go after (behind) the verb or after a preposition *(in, at, on, by, to, etc.)*

Examples

Give it to **John.**	= Give it to **him.**
I see **Mary.**	= I see **her.**
We like **Steven and Mark.**	= We like **them.**
Stand beside **the house.**	= Stand beside **it.**

Exercise 4.16   Answer the questions. Use an object pronoun in your answer.

Example

Do you see **the book** on Mark's desk?
Yes, I see **it.**

1. Are you going to vote for **John?**

   _____

2. Do you like **carrots?**

   _____

3. Are you visiting **your sister** after class today?

   _____

4. Can you hear **your teacher?**

   _____

5. Do you like **cats?**

   _____

6. Do you like **the weather in this city?**

   _____

Possessive adjectives go in front of the noun (or the noun phrase) in the sentence. There is always a noun after a possessive adjective.

Examples

This book belongs to me.	= This is **my** book.
Mary's pencil is over there.	= **Her** pencil is over there.
The desk belongs to Ann and me.	= This is **our** desk.

Possessive pronouns (except "mine") end in "s." (The possessive pronoun form of *it* is rarely used.) They are never followed by the object that is possessed.

Examples

wrong: This is ~~mine~~ book.   **wrong:** That is ~~hers~~ pencil.

right: This book is **mine**.   **right:** That pencil is **hers**.

Exercise 4.17 Use the correct form of the possessive adjective or possessive pronoun in the blanks.

Example

That book belongs to me.   It is ___my___ book.   It is ___mine___ .

1. That coat belongs to him.   It is _____ coat.   It is _____ .

2. Those apples belong to them.   Those are _____ apples.   The apples are

   _____ .

3. This pen belongs to you.   It is _____ pen.   It is _____ .

4. That dog belongs to her.   It is _____ dog.   It is _____ .

5. This lamp belongs to us.   It is _____ lamp.   It is _____ .

The words *this, that, these,* and *those* are called **demonstrative adjectives** when they are followed by a noun, and they are called **demonstrative pronouns** when they are the subject or object of a sentence. *This* (singular) and *these* (plural) are for things that are close to the speaker. *That* (singular) and *those* (plural) are for things that are not close to the speaker.

Examples

That dog is barking. **(over there)**   **Those** dogs are barking. **(over there)**

This dog **(near me)** is not barking.   **These** dogs **(near me)** are not barking.

This is interesting. **(no noun)**   **These** are delicious. **(no noun)**
That is wrong. **(no noun)**   **Those** never arrived. **(no noun)**

Exercise 4.18   Answer the questions. Use an object pronoun in your answer.

Example

Do you see **the book** on Mark's desk?
Yes, I see **it.**

1. Do you have **Arthur's glasses?**

   _____

2. Will you order **the pizza** now?

   _____

3. Will you see **your friend's mother** later?

   _____

4. Does he understand **your father?**

   _____

5. Will you feed **the birds?**

   _____

6. Are you going to visit **your aunt and uncle** tomorrow?

   _____

7. Does your teacher understand **you?**

   _____

8. Do you write to **your father?**

   _____

9. Do you understand **this man?**

   _____

10. Does that woman work with **you and your friend?**

    _____

Exercise 4.19 Let's practice pronouns with a "reciprocal drill." Follow the model, and make the appropriate changes in the sentences. The subject will become the object and vice versa. Notice that sometimes you must make verb changes when changing subjects.

Model

I like (you.) ⟷ You like <u>me</u>.

I borrowed (your) book. ⟷ You borrowed <u>my</u> book.

Example

You have **my** pencil. ___**I** have **your** pencil._____

1. **We** see **him** at the movie. _____

2. **They** have **our** names on the list. _____

3. **She** loves **us**. _____

4. **He** is **their** friend. _____

5. **I** always call **her** on Saturday. _____

6. **You** study with **him**. _____

7. **I** have **your** book. _____

8. **We** liked **her** party. _____

9. **They** study with **us**. _____

Exercise 4.20 Circle the correct form of the demonstrative in each sentence.

1. Do you like (this, these) pens?

2. (That, Those) people are nice.

3. (This, These) is a good idea.

4. (That, Those) are our coats.

5. (That, Those) are my friends.

6. (This, These) is an easy exercise.

7. (That, Those) exams were not easy.

8. (This, These) books are his.

9. We are studying in (this, these) laboratory today.

10. I like (that, those) kind of pizza.

Exercise 4.21 Use *this, that, these,* or *those* in the following sentences:

1. _____ book over there on the desk is not for sale, but _____ one here is.

2. _____ apples here on the table are Pippin. _____ on the kitchen counter are Granny Smith.

3. Is _____ answer on my page here correct?

4. _____ exercise is not that difficult at all.

Exercise 4.22 Substitute most (but not all) of the **boldfaced** words in the paragraph below with pronouns and possessive adjectives.

(1) **Julio Iglesias** _____ is one of the most popular singers in the world today.

(2) **Julio Iglesias** _____ is popular with people from around the world. First of all,

(3) **Julio Iglesias** _____ sings songs in many different languages, which means

that people from many different countries can enjoy (4) **Julio Iglesias'** _____

wonderful romantic voice. Another reason for (5) **Julio Iglesias'** _____ popularity

is the fact that (6) **Julio Iglesias** _____ appeals to women of all ages. (7) **Julio**

Iglesias _____ has a face that is neither young nor old, so most women find (8)

Julio Iglesias _____ attractive. Also, (9) **Julio Iglesias** _____ prefers to

sing romantic songs that appeal to the heart and soul, as well as famous traditional songs

from different countries that are already familiar and well-loved. Most people are in the

mood to hear (10) **Julio Iglesias'** _____ style of song at least once in a while. In

my opinion, (11) **Julio Iglesias** _____ is the most romantic Spanish singer that has

ever lived.

Did you change the last sentence (the conclusion)? Why not?

Sit with a classmate to do this exercise. Cover side A, and ask your partner to cover side B. Ask your partner question #1. Your partner must use pronouns to answer. He/she should tell you the sentence that is in parentheses or one that is similar to it. If your partner has an answer that is very different from the one in parentheses, or if he/she forgets to use pronouns, tell him/her to try again. Let him/her try two times, and then give the answer. Take turns with the items.

A

1. Do you like this class?
   (Yes, **I** like **it**.)
   or (No, **I** don't like **it**.)

2. Does your father live with you?
   (Yes, **he** lives with **me**.)
   (No, **he** does not live with **me**.)

3. Do you see that desk?
   (Yes, **I** see **it**.)
   or (No, **I** don't see **it**.)

4. Do you have the book for me?
   (Yes, **I** have **it** for **you**.)
   or (No, **I** don't have **it** for **you**.)

5. Is your best friend in the United States?
   (Yes, **she/he** is in the United States.)
   or (No, **she/he** is not in the U.S.)

6. Do you want my pencil?
   (No, **I** don't want **your** pencil [or **it**].)
   or (Yes, **I** want **your** pencil [or **it**].)

7. Does this college have good scholarships?
   (Yes, **it** has **them**.)
   or (No, **it** doesn't have **them**.)

8. Is this exercise easy for you?
   (Yes, **it** is easy for **me**.)
   or (No, **it** isn't easy for **me**.)

B

1. Do you study with me after class?
   (No, **I** don't study with **you** after class.)
   or (Yes, **I** study with **you** after class.)

2. Does your mother live with you?
   (Yes, **she** lives with **me**.)
   (No, **she** does not live with **me**.)

3. Do those students see me?
   (Yes, **they** see **you**.)
   or (No, **they** don't see **you**.)

4. Does your professor teach reading to you?
   (No, **she/he** doesn't teach **it** to **me**.)
   or (Yes, **she/he** teaches **it** to **me**.)

5. Are your cousins here at school?
   (Yes, **they** are here at school.)
   or (No, **they** are not here at school.)

6. Do you need my dictionary?
   (Yes, **I** need **your** dictionary [or **it**].)
   or (No, **I** don't need **your** dictionary [or **it**].)

7. Does your best friend write letters to you?

   (Yes, **she/he** writes **them** to **me**.)
   or (No, **she/he** doesn't write **them** to **me**.)

8. Is this exercise difficult for you?
   (No, **it** isn't difficult for **me**.)
   or (Yes, **it** is difficult for **me**.)

ASSIGNMENT

Write a paragraph about a famous singer or actor from your own country. You can use the paragraph about Julio Iglesias as a model if you want. When you finish, exchange paragraphs with a classmate and underline all of the pronouns and possessive adjectives you can find.

Exercise 4.23 Fill in the blanks with the correct pronoun or possessive adjective. Then change the following paragraph to third person singular by changing the subject from *I* to *Sally*.

Example

I live in Kendall with my husband and son.

_____ *Sally (or She) lives in Kendall with her husband and son.* _____

____I____ live in Kendall with ___my___ husband and son. _____ have a large house because _____ husband has _____ business in the house. _____ are a very busy family. _____ son studies in Winston Park Elementary School.

_____ study at Miami-Dade Community College in the morning and work with _____ husband in the afternoon. In the house, _____ answer the telephone for _____ husband's business. _____ take the messages for _____ and return calls. _____ type _____ correspondence and write _____ bills.

After _____ finish with _____ work, _____ have a little time to study. Then _____ pick _____ son up at school and cook dinner for _____ . _____ can see that _____ life is very busy.

Exercise in Error Analysis Do this exercise with a partner. Circle the errors in the following paragraph, and then rewrite the paragraph correctly.

Idania (live) in Wisconsin with (hers) family, she don't has a large house. She have a small townhouse with two bedroom and one bathroom. Idania is a very busy family. She study at the University of Wisconsin in the morning. She don't work. She help her mother with the house in the afternoon and study in the evening. She does all the time she need to study so she a good students.

_____

_____

_____

_____

_____

_____

Exercise 4.24 Fill in or circle the correct form of the word in parentheses.

1. Marie *(live)* __lives__ in Kendall with *(possessive adj.)* __her__ family.

    (subject/pronoun) _____ *(have,* neg.) _____ a large house. She *(have)*

    _____ a small townhouse.

2. *(possessive adj.)* __My__ name is Leyla Flores. I *(work)* _____ at Kendall

    Hospital on the weekends. I *(have)* _____ three children: two boys and one

    girl. *(possessive adj.)* _____ husband is an engineer. He *(has/is)* 40 years

    old. I *(live)* _____ in Kendall near Miami-Dade Community College. I *(take)*

    _____ English classes Monday to Friday from 8:20 AM to 3:15 PM. I *(need)*

    _____ to learn English quickly.

3. *(This, These)* students didn't pass *(this, these)* exam. I think *(this, these)* questions were too difficult. Listen to *(this, these)* two.

4. *(This, That, It)* boat looks like it is going to sink. *(They, Those, That)* waves are too high. I hope it doesn't sink. *(That, Those)* would be terrible. Do you know who *(that, those, it)* belongs to? I think *(it, that, those)* belongs to Ivan.

Exercise 4.25 Circle the subject pronouns, underline the object pronouns, and put a box around the possessive adjectives in the following paragraph.

(We) love to go camping with [our] neighbors, the Salmeróns. (We) usually invite <u>them</u> in January when the weather in Florida is cool. Peace River is our favorite place to camp. We love it because when we go there, we always camp far away from other people. When we go to Peace River, we seldom go to a campground. We always take our canoes with us and ride down the river in them until we see a place that we like. Then we set up our tents and go hiking or fishing. In the afternoon, we play badminton, volleyball, and frisbee. Denise Salmerón is a very good cook, and she loves to fry the fish we catch. She serves them to us on paper plates. José Salmerón and his girls go with us into the forest to find wood for our fire. We sing camp songs by the campfire at night and sleep in our cozy little tents. We always go camping at least two times a year with our neighbors, and we always have a wonderful time with them.

Exercise 4.26 On a separate piece of paper, rewrite the preceding paragraph. Change it to the third person plural by changing "we" to "they" (the Duráns). Start your new paragraph like this:

The Duráns love to go camping with their neighbors, the Salmeróns.

Exercise 4.27 Write a similar paragraph about your favorite vacation activities. Share your paragraph with a classmate. Tell your classmate what you think of his/her vacation activities, and ask him/her what he/she thinks of your vacation activities.

Exercise 4.28 Interview a classmate about his/her customary vacation activities and write about them. Use "he" or "she" and the corresponding pronouns and possessive adjectives in your paragraph. Use adverbs of frequency in your paragraph if possible.

VOCABULARY BUILDING

Write ten new vocabulary words that you learned in class this week. Next to each word, write a synonym for the word (or the translation for the word in your own language if you cannot find a synonym). Then write the word in a sentence.

1. _____

_____

2. _____

_____

3. _____

_____

4. _____

_____

5. _____

_____

6. _____

_____

7. _____

_____

8. _____

_____

9. _____

_____

10. _____

_____

chapter
five

Describing Places and Objects

■ **STEP ONE**
Select adjectives which develop the controlling ideas.

■ **STEP TWO**
Put adjectives in the correct order in the noun phrase.

■ **STEP THREE**
Use prepositional phrases to give the precise locations of objects and places.

■ **STEP FOUR**
Use *there is/there are* and *it is/they are* to add variety to the paragraph.

The computer program that accompanies this section is called: "Adjectives" (Macintosh and IBM)

ADJECTIVES

After Verbs

Most adjectives describe the way things look, feel, taste, sound, or seem. They can describe the quantity, general appearance, size, shape, condition, age, color, origin, or material (what things are made of). Adjectives are especially important in descriptive paragraphs because they develop the controlling ideas.

Adjectives can go in various places in a sentence. A common position for adjectives is after "linking verbs" such as *be, seem, taste, feel, sound, smell,* and *look.*

Examples Linking verbs appear in *italic,* adjectives appear in **boldfaced** type.

That music *sounds* **awful.**

You *look* **marvelous.**

The soup *smells* **delicious.**

This sandwich *tastes* **peculiar.**

When you use *two* adjectives after a linking verb, use *and* (with no comma) to separate them.

Examples

That music sounds **loud and terrible.**

My father is **kind and generous.**

When you use *more than two* adjectives after a linking verb, use *and* (with a comma before the last adjective) to separate them.

Examples

That soup looks **hot, steamy, and delicious.**

The children feel **tired, cranky, and sleepy.**

Exercise 5.1 Fill in the blanks with any appropriate adjective or adjectives.

1. This class is _____ and _____ .

2. My favorite classmate looks _____ .

3. The teacher sounds _____ today.

4. This lesson seems _____ .

In Noun Phrases

Adjectives can go in front of the noun that they are describing. But be careful! When you put more than two adjectives in front of a noun, you need to know a few rules about their order. In this section, we will begin by looking at the different kinds of adjectives that can go in front of a noun. Notice that they are presented in the order in which they can be placed in noun phrases.

● Predeterminers

Predeterminers are words that go first in front of a noun. Not every noun needs a predeterminer, but if you use a predeterminer and an adjective together, the predeterminer goes first.

all (of)	both (of)	many (of)	some (of)	half (of)
five (of)	several (of)	none (of)	a couple (of)	one (of)

Examples

Several (of the) white mice had long tails.
All (of) the white mice looked identical.

Exercise 5.2 Fill in the blank with an appropriate predeterminer.

1. _____ the people in this school speak my native language.

2. _____ the animals in the zoo are mammals.

● Determiners and Possessives

Determiners and **possessive** words go after any predeterminers before the noun.

the	a	an	his	my	our
her	Jane's	that	this	these	those

Examples

Some of **these** gray marbles are not mine.

My gray marbles are larger than **John's** yellow marbles.

Exercise 5.3 Fill in the blank with an appropriate determiner or possessive word.

1. _____ book is not yours.

2. _____ blue disks are not for this computer.

● Opinion

Adjectives that give a **general opinion** come before the other types of adjectives in a sentence. Most adjectives are in this category.

pretty	ugly	boring	exotic	extravagant
beautiful	nice	challenging	silly	funny

Example

The **cute** little teddy bear came from that **expensive** new store.

Exercise 5.4 Fill in the blank with an appropriate adjective of general opinion.

1. Her _____ smile enchants people.

2. This school's _____ library is a nice place to study.

● Intensifiers

Intensifiers (usually adverbs) can be used as adjectives and can be placed in several places. One of the most common positions for an intensifier is in front of the adjective of general opinion.

very	extremely	a little	quite	intensely

Examples

The **extremely** cold weather made the cat shiver.

The weather was **very** cold last year.

Exercise 5.5   Fill in the blank with an appropriate intensifier.

1. That _____ funny clown works in the circus.

2. The weather in this town in summer is (not?) _____ hot.

• Size

Adjectives that describe **size** come before those that describe shape.

big   small   gigantic   tiny   huge

Example

She needed some very **small** shoes for her cute **little** feet.

Exercise 5.6   Fill in the blank with an appropriate adjective of size.

1. I have _____ feet, but my uncle has _____ feet.

2. People with _____ eyes look nice.

• Shape

Adjectives that describe **shape** come before those that describe condition.

round   circular   square   star-shaped   triangular   rectangular

Example

 The little **round** ball was next to the small **square** box.

Exercise 5.7   Fill in the blank with an appropriate adjective of shape.

1. My _____ computer disk is not in the computer.

2. Mary's large _____ tiles are not Italian.

Condition

Adjectives of **condition** come after adjectives of shape.

broken   strong   ragged   fat   oily   dilapidated   dirty   dry

Example

The big **strong** cat lives in the **dirty** alley behind my house.

Exercise 5.8   Fill in the blank with an appropriate adjective of condition.

1. This _____ classroom needs to be cleaned.

2. Marlene's _____ vase needs to be repaired.

Age

Next come the adjectives that describe **age.**

old   new   young   antique   ancient

Example

My sister's tiny **young** son has just learned to crawl.

Exercise 5.9   Fill in the blank with an appropriate adjective of age.

1. Their _____ baby sleeps all night long.

2. I have just bought a (an) _____ vase that is worth a lot of money.

Color

Color adjectives come after those that describe age.

| white | off-white | reddish | blue-gray |
| light blue | black | navy blue | dark gray |

Example

The small old **blue and gray** house needs some fresh paint.

Exercise 5.10 Fill in the blank with (an) appropriate color adjective(s).

   1. The _____ flag is American.

   2. The _____ ceiling in this room is (not?) very clean.

● Origin or Material

Adjectives that tell the **origin** or **material** of the noun are next.

  French   German   plastic   wooden   brick

Example

The red **brick** wall needs to be washed.

Exercise 5.11 Fill in the blank with an appropriate adjective of origin or material.

   1. George is a handsome young _____ soccer player.

   2. Her new _____ dish melted in the dishwasher.

● Noun Adjuncts

The last adjective that comes in front of a noun is another **noun** (noun adjunct) that is being used as an adjective to describe the noun.

   water (water hydrant)   flower (flower pot)   house (house party)   car (car port)

Example

The small new **alarm** clock keeps good time.

Exercise 5.12 Fill in the blank with an appropriate noun adjunct.

   1. A disk for a computer is called a _____ .

   2. A station for fires is called a _____ .

It is not good to use too many adjectives in front of the noun. However, when you need to use more than one descriptive adjective in a sentence, you must respect their order. The following sentence sounds absurd because there are too many adjectives to describe "car."

    One of his very ugly small square broken old gray plastic toy cars is under the kitchen table.

COORDINATE ADJECTIVES

If you use more than one adjective of the same category (general opinion, color, size, and so on) in the same noun phrase, they are called **coordinate adjectives,**[1] and you need to separate them with a comma.

Examples

She has an **strange, exotic** smile. (Both adjectives are general opinions.)

This is a **red, white, and blue** flag. (All three are adjectives of color.)

Exercise 5.13 Box the words in the following sentences that are out of order and then place an arrow where they should be in the sentence.

Example

Half of John's ⬇ old valuable books are on the ⬇ bookshelf wooden.

1. Cake chocolate is better than cake vanilla.
2. Please pass me some of that new delicious French pastry.
3. The pile large of laundry dirty was in the corner of her room.
4. The teacher writing was late to the class English today because her old ugly car broke down on the freeway.
5. The green and blue new sweater looks very nice on her.
6. Her brother young was in the army for ten years.

Exercise 5.14 Put the words in parentheses in the correct order, and then write a complete sentence with those words.

predeterminer	determiner	intensifier	opinion	size	shape
condition	age	color	origin/material	noun adjunct	

Example

rectangular brown window (add "strange")

  strange rectangular brown window

  The strange rectangular brown window is broken.

---

1 Coordinate adjectives are adjectives whose location in the sentence can be changed without changing the meaning of the sentence.

1. rectangular brown window (add "ugly")

   _____

   _____

2. rectangular brown windows (add "my father's")

   _____

   _____

3. rectangular brown window (add "unusual" and "very")

   _____

   _____

4. silly blue hats (add "old," "small," and "many of")

   _____

   _____

5. silly blue hats (add "torn," "many," and "old")

   _____

   _____

6. silly blue hats (add "none of the," and "round")

   _____

   _____

Exercise 5.15 Put the words in correct order. Then finish the sentence logically with your own words.

predeterminer	determiner	intensifier	opinion	size	shape
condition	age	color	origin/material	noun adjunct	

Example

his / some of / tests / very / difficult

Some of his very difficult tests frustrate the students in this class.

1. Mary's / all of / clothes / extremely / expensive

_____

2. one of / friends / my / best

_____

3. Heather's / some of / shirts / new / white

_____

4. handsome / small / the / man

_____

5. exotic / that / Iranian / dancer

_____

6. leather / handbag / brown / one of / Janet's

_____

7. Peruvian / seafood / dish / that / unusual

_____

8. very / funny / Italian / old / professor / my

_____

9. the / interesting / books / French / old / very / one of

_____

10. cats / small / white / one of / Mary's

_____

Exercise 5.16 Do this exercise with a partner. Use a concept map to plan a descriptive paragraph for the scene below. Use as many descriptive adjectives as you can (both in noun phrases and after linking verbs) in your paragraph. Be sure to use connecting words in your paragraph.

SPATIAL SEQUENCE IN PARAGRAPHS DESCRIBING PLACES

When you describe a place, remember that your reader will see everything in the order that you present the details of your paragraph. After you plan the supporting details, you must organize them so that the reader will visualize your scene in a logical (or even a dramatic) sequence. Prepositions of location and the expressions *there is, there are, it is,* and *they are* can be useful for this purpose. Prepositional phrases give the precise location of objects, and *there is/are* is used to add variety to the types of sentences you write. Notice how the paragraph from the warm-up exercise is improved by adding a simple point of reference: "around me."

It is a beautiful day at the beach. There are hundreds of fluffy white clouds in the sky. It is sunny, but there is a cool ocean breeze blowing gently. There are large blue waves moving slowly toward the shore. It is very easy today to feel peaceful and relaxed here at the beach.

It is a beautiful day at the beach. **Above me,** there are hundreds of fluffy white clouds in the sky. It is sunny, but there is a cool ocean breeze blowing gently **through my hair. In front of me,** there are large blue waves moving slowly toward the shore. It is very easy today to feel peaceful and relaxed here at the beach!

When you plan your paragraph describing a place, pretend that your eye is a camera that is recording what other people will watch. If your camera jumps suddenly from one place to another, your movie will be confusing (and probably annoying), but if your camera focuses on essential details in a logical sequence, your movie and your message (the controlling idea) will be clear to the viewer. This method of organizing the details of your paragraphs is called "spatial sequence." It is a sequential presentation of the place that you are describing.

Read and **view in your mind** the scene described in the following paragraphs. Which of the two paragraphs is easier to see in your mind? Why?

This living room is a horrible mess. The floor is dirty. There is a pile of books in a corner. Dirty dishes are on the table. The furniture is dusty. There are clothes, papers, and stacks of old books in a corner. The windows are brown with dirt. Marks are on the wall. The people who live here need to hire a cleaning service.

This living room is a horrible mess. As you walk into the room, the first thing you see are piles of things everywhere. In the corner to your right there is a pile of clothes. In the opposite corner there is a pile of books, and between those two corners, the floor is covered with clothes, papers, and stacks of old books. The walls and windows in this room are also dirty and stained, and the furniture and floor in front of the window are covered with dust. The people who live in this dirty house need to hire a cleaning service.

Exercise 5.17 Describe your location in the classroom by filling in the blanks with appropriate names of classmates and objects. Write **three** additional sentences to complete the description of your classroom.

I am sitting between _____ and _____ .

_____ is in front of me, and _____ is behind me.

On the walls there (is, are) _____ and _____ .

The teacher is in front of the _____ . Next to the teacher there

(is, are) _____ .

1. _____

2. _____

3. _____

Prepositions of Location

The computer programs that accompany this section are called: "Building Sentences" (Macintosh) and "Complete Sentences" (IBM), and they contain a short tutorial on one-word prepositions of location.

Prepositions of location tell where objects are located. (Prepositions of location include: *in, between, behind, near, next to, beside, on, above, over, at, under, below, among,* and *through-out.*) They are essential in paragraphs that describe places and things, and they can even help a description of a person become more interesting. Look at the following sentences and *circle the prepositions in each example.*

The egg is in the skillet.

Your class is next to mine.

They put the homework on the professor's desk.

You are among friends.

The post office is near the bank.

They parked beside my car.

The clock is above the picture.

That desert is below sea level.

To describe the location of a thing that is **inside** of another thing, use *the.*

Examples

The office is **in back of** the house. = The office is a separate building, and that building is located behind the house.

The office is **in the back of** the house. = The office is a room inside the house (in the back part of the house).

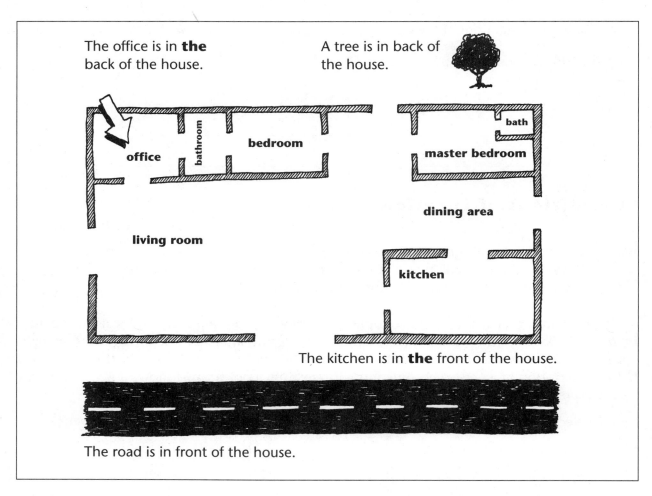

The office is in **the** back of the house.

A tree is in back of the house.

bath

bathroom

bedroom

master bedroom

office

dining area

living room

kitchen

The kitchen is in **the** front of the house.

The road is in front of the house.

Exercise 5.18 Answer the following questions. Pay attention to the word *the* in your answers.

1. What rooms are in the front of your house?

_____

2. What is in front of your house?

_____

3. How many bedrooms are in the back of your house?

_____

4. How many trees are in back of your house?

_____

The preposition *across* can be used two ways:

1. Naming the object (or obstacle) that separates the two places you are describing

   Example

   Mark sits **across THE ROOM from** me.

2. Not naming that object

   Example

   Mark sits **across from** me.

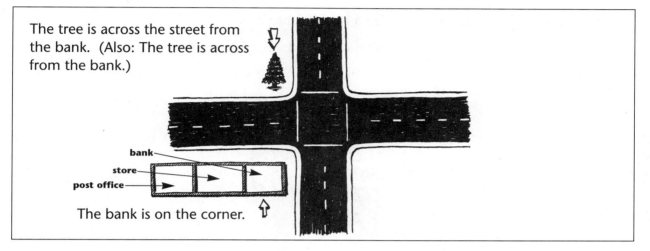

The tree is across the street from the bank. (Also: The tree is across from the bank.)

bank

store

post office

The bank is on the corner.

Exercise 5.19 Discuss the use of prepositions in the following diagram. Explain the difference between "on the corner" (above) and "in the corner" (below).

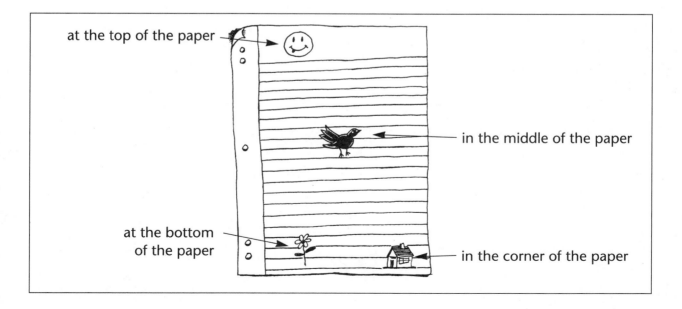

at the top of the paper

in the middle of the paper

at the bottom of the paper

in the corner of the paper

Exercise 5.20   Do this exercise with a partner. Follow the instructions 1–5 and answer the questions 6–20 in complete sentences.

1. Put an "X" **in the center of** this box and a "Y" **under** the "X."

2. Put a circle **below** the "Y" and a square **above** the "X."

3. Write your teacher's name **on** the box and your father's name **near** it.

4. **Beside** your teacher's name, write the name of your favorite author.

5. Write the name of your favorite actor **above** the name of your favorite author.

5.27

6. Where is the computer?

_____

7. Where is the telephone?

_____

8. Where is the man?

_____

9. Where is the paper?

_____

10. Where is the chair?

_____

11. Where is this man?

_____

12. Where is the horse?

_____

13. Where is the church?

_____

14. Where is the window?

_____

15. Where is the chef?

_____

16. Where are the tables?

_____

17. Where are the chandeliers?

_____

18. Where is the umbrella?

_____

19. Where is the man?

_____

20. Where is the gas station attendant?

_____

Exercise 5.21 Use the concept map below to fill in the blanks with the correct prepositions of location in the following paragraph. (The prepositional phrases in the concept map are NOT complete sentences. You must add words to them.)

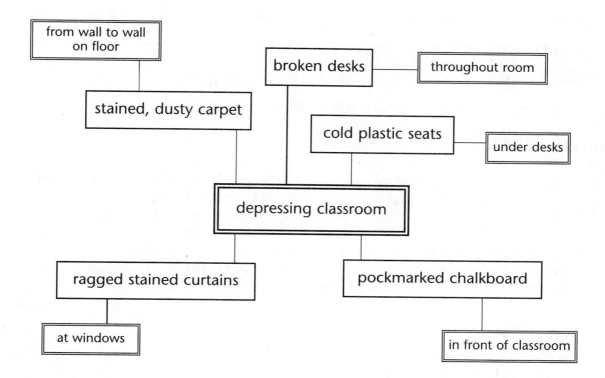

Our writing class is held _____ the most depressing classroom _____ campus. The dark room has two ragged stained curtains hanging _____ the dirty gray window _____ the door. The dark desks, many of which are broken, are scattered _____ the room in messy rows, and a cold plastic seat is attached to each ugly desk. _____ of the classroom, there is a greenish pockmarked chalkboard. There is a stained, dusty carpet _____ the floor. _____ a classroom like this, it is very hard to concentrate on lessons.

Exercise 5.22 Add prepositions and prepositional phrases to this paragraph explaining where the objects are located.

In my house, my favorite room is my bedroom. _____ , I have

softly colored floral decorations that make my bedroom pleasant and relaxing. A large

mirror is _____ and a huge window is _____ .

They both add depth to the room and make it look bright and cheerful. I also love my oak

desk, which is _____ and the matching chair _____ .

My bedroom always helps me feel relaxed and cheerful.

Exercise 5.23

Part 1 Find (or draw on a separate piece of paper) a picture of an unusual-looking person, and use a concept map to write a paragraph describing the features (AND THE LOCATION OF THE FEATURES) that make the person/people look so unusual.

Part 2 Read your description to a partner in the class. As you read, your partner will try to draw what you describe. When your partner has finished the drawing, show him/her the original picture you described.

Exercise 5.24

After you complete the paragraph for Exercise 5.23, your homework is to describe your living room. Use prepositional phrases to describe the location of each item you describe.

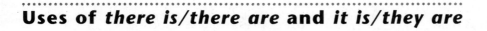

Uses of *there is/there are* and *it is/they are*

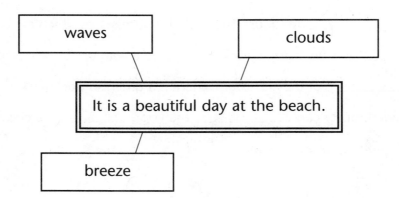

Fill in the blanks with *there is, there are, it is,* and *they are.* (Check your answers on page 120.)

_____ a beautiful day at the beach. Above me, _____

_____ hundreds of fluffy white clouds in the sky. _____

sunny, but _____ a cool breeze blowing gently from the ocean.

_____ large blue waves moving slowly toward the shore.

_____ very easy today to feel peaceful and relaxed here at the beach!

Every verb (except the imperative) in an English sentence needs a subject. Sometimes, there is no logical subject for a verb, so we use the subject *there* with the verb *be* to indicate a location or the existence of something. *There* doesn't usually refer to anything. It is in the sentence because there must be a subject for the verb *be*. Sometimes, the word *there* refers to the noun that follows *is* or *are*. In those cases, the expression is used to add a variety to the types of sentences used in the paragraph.

The plural form, *there are,* is usually followed by an expression of quantity such as *some, a lot of, many, five, six.*

Examples

There is not enough time to do this.

There are many ways to cook an egg.

Be sure not to confuse *there is* with *it is*. *It is* used for **weather, temperature, time, distance,** or as a **pronoun** referring to a specific thing.

Examples

It is sunny (rainy, foggy, breezy) today. **(weather)**

It is hot (cold, freezing, cool, warm) today. **(temperature)**

It is three o'clock (noon, midnight, 5:30). **(time)**

It is five miles (20 blocks, two kilometers) to Flagler Street from here. **(distance)**

The flower is pretty.   **It** is pretty. **(it = the flower)**

The apple is a Granny Smith.   **It** is a Granny Smith. **(it = the apple)**

The book is on the table.   **It** is on the table. **(it = the book)**

Forms of *there is* and *there are*

affirmative:

There is a dog under this table. **(singular)**

There are some pencils on the desk. **(plural)**

contraction:

There's a dog under this table. **(singular)**

(There's NO written contraction for **There + are**)

negative:

There is not a cat.

There are not any cats.

negative contraction:

There isn't a cat under this table. **(singular)**

There's not a cat under this table. **(singular)**

There aren't any pencils on the desk. **(plural)**

yes-no questions and short answers:

Is there a bookstore on campus?

Yes, **there is.**

Are there scholarships available for residents?

Yes, **there are.**

information questions:

How many Spaniards **are there** in this class?

tag questions:

There are some apples in the bowl, **aren't there?**

There is a name for that dance, **isn't there?**

Exercise 5.25 Use *there is, there are, it is,* or *they are* in the following blanks. Note that some of the sentences are questions.

1. _____ a blackboard in this classroom. _____ large and clean?

2. _____ many students in the room? Yes, and _____ from different countries.

3. _____ good weather in Miami? Well, _____ usually hot and sunny.

4. _____ late? _____ 3:00 PM.

5. _____ nine buildings on campus. _____ all large?

6. _____ not far from here to the post office. _____ across the street from the school.

Exercise 5.26   Circle the correct words in the parentheses in the following paragraph.

Our classroom is designed to make learning easy. In it, (there, it, they) (is, are) twenty-five comfortable desks. (There, It, They) (is, are) in a semicircle in the middle of the room, so everyone in the class can see everyone else in the class. In the front of the classroom, (there, it, they) (is, are) two large chalkboards that all students can see clearly. (There, It, They) (is, are) also a table between the chalkboard and the desks. That (is, are) the place where the teacher puts the students' handouts. (There, It, They) (is, are) a brown table with an odd shape, neither square nor rectangle. (There, It, They) (is, are) six walls in the classroom, and that is unusual. (There, It, They) (is, are) usually only four walls in a room. (There, It, They) (is, are) interesting to see so many walls in this room. (There, It, They) (is, are) two overhead projectors, a computer, and a television set in class, too. The teacher uses them to explain the lessons. (They, There, It) (is, are) in front of the desk. I like this room. (There, It) (is, are) comfortable.

Exercise 5.27   Now read the above paragraph again with a classmate, and cross out the sentences that do not develop the controlling idea "designed to make learning easy." Add any necessary details to make the paragraph sound complete.

Exercise 5.28

Part 1 Look at the following picture. With a classmate, write a paragraph describing this house. Decide on a controlling idea for your paragraph before you begin your concept map. Use *there is, there are, it is,* and *they are* in your sentences.

Part 2 Exchange your paragraph with another pair of students in the class, and check their paragraph for the following:

1. Does their paragraph have a topic sentence? __ Yes __ No

   a. What is the focused topic in the topic sentence? _____

   b. What is the controlling idea in the topic sentence? _____

2. How many supporting sentences are in their paragraph? __

(If there are three supporting sentences in the body, continue to the next questions. If there are fewer than three supporting sentences, return the paragraph to the owner and tell him/her to write three supports in the body.)

3. In the second sentence,[2] what aspect is described? _____

4. In the second sentence, what adjectives are used? _____

5. In the third sentence, what aspect is described? _____

6. In the third sentence, what adjectives are used? _____

7. In the fourth sentence, what aspect is described? _____

8. In the fourth sentence, what adjectives are used? _____

9. Is there a conclusion? __ Yes __ No

   a. If "yes,"

      Does the conclusion restate the focused topic? __ Yes __ No

      What kind of conclusion is it?

         ___ advice or invitation

         ___ opinion

         ___ restatement of the topic sentence

         ___ summary

   b. If "no," write one for their paragraph.

   _____

   _____

10. Return paragraphs to the original writers, and discuss your evaluations.

---

2 The second sentence of the body is the first main supporting sentence.

Write ten new vocabulary words that you learned in class this week. Next to each word, write the translation for the word in your own language. Then write the word in a sentence.

1. _____

_____

2. _____

_____

3. _____

_____

4. _____

_____

5. _____

_____

6. _____

_____

7. _____

_____

8. _____

_____

9. _____

_____

10. _____

_____

1. How do you feel about your grades in this class?

   _____

2. Do you know how well you are doing in this class?

   _____

3. What kinds of evaluations does your teacher give you? Does it help you? Do you want more tests? More writing assignments?

   _____

4. What kinds of evaluations and feedback would you like to have from your teacher on the writing assignments in this class?

   _____

5. How does your teacher let you know when you have a problem in writing?

   _____

chapter
six

Process Paragraphs—Part 1

MODEL PARAGRAPH AND OVERVIEW

Writing a process paragraph involves five steps:

■ **STEP ONE**
Write the topic sentence.

■ **STEP TWO**
List the support for your topic sentence.

■ **STEP THREE**
Put the supporting sentences in chronological order.

■ **STEP FOUR**
Connect the supporting sentences with connecting words.

■ **STEP FIVE**
Write the conclusion.

In previous chapters, you learned to develop an academic paragraph of description, and the grammar you studied helped you to develop different aspects of a descriptive paragraph. In the next two chapters, you are going to learn to write **process paragraphs.** You will see how to write topic sentences, how to plan and write the body, and how to conclude paragraphs that explain how to do or make something. You will learn how process paragraphs are different from descriptive paragraphs. You will also learn the grammar and sentence structures that you can use to write this new type of paragraph.

In this chapter you will study the **imperative,** or **command** form, of verbs. Commands are very common in process paragraphs, especially in paragraphs that describe detailed processes, because they communicate essential information with a minimum of words. After you learn the imperative, you will learn some **present tense modal auxiliaries.** Modals add an authoritative tone to a paragraph.

In Chapter 7, you will learn some more sentence connectors which help to describe a sequence of events in chronological order (Step 4 of writing process paragraphs). These connectors will be **subordinating conjunctions** (*when, while, after, as,* etc.) and **transitional words and expressions** (*first of all, next, afterwards, also,* etc.). These sentence connectors make the supporting sentences in your paragraph sound organized and logically related to each other.

WRITING PROCESS PARAGRAPHS

A process paragraph is a paragraph such as the one below that explains in detail HOW to do or make something. The length of the process paragraph depends upon the topic you select. If the paragraph seems to be too long, focus the topic more, or select a different topic.

Fill in the blanks as your teacher reads this paragraph to you.

It is easy to write a (1) _____ paragraph (2) _____ you follow these

(3) _____ . (4) _____ _____ _____ , you (5) _____

select a topic. The topic (6) _____ be something that you know how to do and

that requires a step-by-step procedure. (7) _____ , you (8) _____ plan the

support of your paragraph. The support in a process paragraph is (9) _____ lim-

ited to three ideas (10) _____ most processes have more than three steps. To

(11) _____ the support, you (12) _____ make a list of all the steps that the

process requires, (13) _____ _____ put the steps in chronological order.

(14) _____ you check the list to see that all of the important (15) _____ are

in the correct order and that all essential details are included, you (16) _____ write

your first draft of the paragraph. As you write your support sentences, you (17)

_____ use connecting words such as (18) _____ , (19) _____ , (20)

_____ , (21) _____ , (22) _____ , (23) _____ , and (24)

_____ . These words will help your reader follow your (25) _____ and will

help you keep your steps (26) _____ . (27) _____ you finish the support,

you are finally ready to write your conclusion. The conclusion (28) _____ be an

(29) _____ to the reader to follow your advice, a brief restatement of the major

steps, or a (30) _____ not to deviate from the steps you have described.

Sometimes the (31) _____ itself is a conclusion; for example, the last step in a

recipe would be to serve the food and enjoy it. As you can see, it is (32) _____

_____ to write a process paragraph, (33) _____ you just (34) _____ it,

(35) _____ it, and (36) _____ it for essential details.

Discuss the following questions about the preceding paragraph with a partner.

1. How many sentences are usually in an academic paragraph of description?

   _____

2. How many sentences are in the paragraph? _____

3. Why are there so many sentences in a process paragraph?

4. How are the supporting sentences organized?

5. What does the conclusion of the paragraph do? (give advice? summarize? warn? invite?)

The Topic Sentence

The topic sentence of a process paragraph tells the reader the topic of the paragraph, which in this case is the process you are going to describe. The controlling idea informs the reader that your paragraph is one of process, and maybe that the process is "easy" or "not difficult" (or maybe "difficult but not impossible"), "fun," "exciting," "important," or "challenging." A popular type of topic sentence for a process paragraph is one that says something interesting about the topic and catches the reader's attention.

Examples

It is **easy** to wash a dog if you follow **these five steps.**

It is **not easy** to change a tire, but if you follow **these instructions** carefully, you should be able to do it.

To cook the perfect "paella," it is important to follow **these instructions** very carefully.

Contrary to what most people believe, formatting a computer disk is **not difficult** if you can remember **four basic steps.**

Exercise 6.1 Using the sample sentences at the beginning of this section as examples, create topic sentences with the following elements:

1. cooking spaghetti / easy / five steps

2. easy / to make / paper airplane / these steps

3. not difficult / play Monopoly / this process

4. to register for classes / not impossible / these simple steps

5. painting a house / hard but not impossible / prepare the walls properly

Exercise 6.2 Which of the following topics is too general for a paragraph of process? Focus the topics that are too general.

	Too General?	Corrected Focused Topic (if needed)
1. Change the oil in a car	Y __ N __	_____
2. Repair a car	Y __ N __	_____
3. Cook pancakes	Y __ N __	_____
4. Make ceramics	Y __ N __	_____
5. Play cards	Y __ N __	_____

Exercise 6.3   With a partner focus the following topics and then write a topic sentence for **process** paragraphs using your focused topic. Make sure that all of your topic sentences would introduce a paragraph that describes HOW TO do something. You do not need to write these paragraphs now.

1. Education _____

2. Computers _____

3. Food _____

4. Vacation _____

5. Books _____

The Body

A good first step in planning the body of a process paragraph is to write the steps of the process as a list. While you are making the list, you do not need to put the steps in strict chronological order. Simply write down all of the steps you can think of for the process you are describing. A list of steps for washing a dog, for example, might look like this:

wet the dog
put soap on the dog
cut the dog's hair
put a leash on the dog
brush the dog
rinse the soap off the dog
dry the dog
take the dog outside
clip the dog's toenails
scrub the dog

After you have the list of steps for the process, you next put them in chronological order. At this time, you can eliminate any of the steps that are illogical or unnecessary. Now your list might look like this:

___3___ wet the dog

___4___ put soap on the dog

_____ ~~cut the dog's hair~~

___1___ put a leash on the dog

___8___ brush the dog

___6___ rinse the soap off the dog

___7___ dry the dog

___2___ take the dog outside

_____ ~~clip the dog's toenails~~

___5___ scrub the dog

After you have your steps in chronological order and have eliminated all of the unnecessary steps, you are ready to add more details to your list. Now your list might look like this:

___3___ wet the dog   start with the head and finish with the tail

___4___ put soap on the dog   be careful with the eyes

_____ ~~cut the dog's hair~~

___1___ put a leash on the dog

___8___ brush the dog   to make its coat shine

___6___ rinse the soap off the dog   be sure to get all the soap off

___7___ dry the dog   or let the dog shake to dry itself

___2___ take the dog outside

_____ ~~clip the dog's toenails~~

___5___ scrub the dog

Now you have all the steps of your process, they are in chronological order, and you have details to make your paragraph interesting. You have eliminated the unnecessary steps and are now ready to write the support sentences of the body.

The body of the process paragraph must give all of the important steps of the process in chronological order. This means that you will probably have more than three supporting sentences in the process paragraph. You cannot leave out any of the important steps, and you cannot write them out of sequence—they must be given in the order in which they occur. If you make a mistake in the order, the reader will not understand the process, and if he/she tries to duplicate it, he/she will fail (and will probably be angry with you).

Exercise 6.4 With a classmate, write a paragraph using the final list for "washing a dog."

_____

_____

_____

_____

_____

_____

Exercise 6.5 With a partner, determine which of the steps in the three processes below are NOT needed and cross them out. Then put the remaining steps in the most logical chronological order for the process. Add any details you can think of to make each process very clear. Finally, select one of the processes, and write a paragraph including all of the steps.

1. Topic: Preparing for an international trip
   Topic sentence: Traveling to other countries can be exciting, and if you prepare
                    for it correctly, your trip will go smoothly.

   ___ Find the lowest priced tickets.

   ___ Get passports.

   ___ Pack bags.

   ___ Chewing gum helps during take-offs and landings.

   ___ Buy some foreign currency.

   ___ Buy traveler's checks.

   ___ Make hotel reservations.

   ___ Buy the plane tickets.

2. Topic: Preparing for a dinner party
   Topic sentence: The success of a formal dinner party depends upon proper planning.

   __ Determine time and place and number of guests.

   __ Buy food/drinks.

   __ Determine whom to invite.

   __ Prepare the house with decorations.

   __ Wash the windows.

   __ Arrange entertainment.

   __ Determine theme for the party.

   __ Turn off the television.

   __ Send invitations.

   __ Prepare the food and drinks.

   __ Dress for the party.

   __ Buy a birthday cake.

Exercise 6.6 Find classmates who know how to change the oil in a car. If possible, sit in groups where at least one person understands this process. Do the following exercise together. The person who knows how to change oil in a car will explain any of the steps you do not understand.

In the following paragraph, circle the step in the support that is out of order.

It is important to change the oil in your car frequently to keep your car running well. Before you begin, you must buy five quarts of oil and an oil filter. You must also have a special tool to unscrew the oil filter, a wrench to unscrew the bolt on the oil drain, and a pan to catch the oil as it drains. Let the engine sit for about fifteen minutes while the new oil filter absorbs a quart of oil, and then add the fifth quart of oil to the engine. After you have these items, you are ready to begin. First, put the drain pan under the oil drain and remove the screw. After all of the oil drains into this pan, you should dispose of it carefully so it does not contaminate the environ-ment. Next, you are ready to remove the oil filter. Place the tool around the filter and turn the tool counterclockwise until the filter comes loose. At this point, you must replace the screw to the oil drain, screw on the new oil filter, and add four quarts of oil. Now you are ready to drive again, this time with a cleaner, smoother-running engine.

Exercise 6.7 In the following paragraph, circle the step in the support that is out of order.

It is easy to cut your little girl's hair if you follow these steps. Then you should divide the hair into different sections and pin each section up, except for the hair that is on the back of the head at the bottom. First of all, you need to wet the hair and comb it. Next, you put your comb in one hand, your scissors in the other, and use them both together to start cutting the hair that you left down at the back of the head. As soon as you have cut the first section of hair, use it as a pattern to cut the next section, and then the next. Continue until all the hair on the head is cut the same length. As you can see, it is easy to cut hair, and you can save money if you learn to do it yourself.

Exercise 6.8 Develop lists to plan the support for these topics. (First brainstorm for the steps. Then organize the steps chronologically, add details, and eliminate the unnecessary steps.)

1. Registering for classes

_____

_____

_____

_____

_____

_____

2. Buying books at the school bookstore

_____

_____

_____

_____

_____

_____

The Conclusion

The conclusion of a process paragraph may be an invitation for the reader to try the process, a humorous suggestion, a brief summary of the main steps of the process, an opinion, or some advice.

Examples

As you can see, washing a dog is not so hard to do if you follow these simple and logical steps. **(restates the topic sentence)**

After washing, rinsing, and drying your dog, you are now ready to enjoy a good game of fetch with your clean, happy pet. **(gives brief summary of the important steps)**

You can see, then, that washing a dog is not a complicated process; however, it can be even easier—if you can get your sister or brother to do it for you. **(humorous invitation)**

It is best to wash your dog at least once every two weeks in hot weather. **(one last word of advice)**

Exercise 6.9   Pick four of the paragraphs presented in this chapter. You may use the example paragraphs that are in the chapter or paragraphs that you and your partner have written in the exercises. Write two different conclusions for each of the paragraphs.

1. Original conclusion: _____

   _____

   New conclusion A: _____

   _____

   New conclusion B: _____

   _____

2. Original conclusion: _____

   _____

   New conclusion A: _____

   _____

   New conclusion B: _____

   _____

3. Original conclusion: _____

_____

New conclusion A: _____

_____

New conclusion B: _____

_____

4. Original conclusion: _____

_____

New conclusion A: _____

_____

New conclusion B: _____

_____

Sentence Structures for Process Paragraphs

Dictation Pay special attention to imperatives, modal auxiliaries, and connecting words in the following dictation:

(1) _____ _____ only five steps that you (2) _____ remember when you want to tape a program from your television set onto your videocassette recorder (VCR). (3) _____ , insert a blank tape in the VCR and rewind it. You (4) _____ use a good quality tape when you record so it (5) _____ break inside your VCR. (6) _____ , set the channel on your VCR to the channel you want to record. This does not (7) _____ _____ be the channel you are watching on the television. (8) _____ the program is about to begin, (9) _____ the *record* and *play* buttons on your VCR. You do not (10) _____ _____ have your television turned on to record a program on the VCR. Turn off the VCR (11) _____

the program is over, rewind the tape, (12) _____ watch it on Channel 3 or 4 of your television. (13) _____ you (14) _____ these five simple (15) _____ , you will have no problems recording your second favorite program while watching your favorite program at the same time.

• • • • • • • • • •
IMPERATIVES

The *imperative* (also called the *command* form) is frequently used in process paragraphs, especially in paragraphs written to instruct people about how to do or make something. To form an imperative, or command, use the base form of the verb. You do not need to write a subject in an imperative sentence because the subject for all imperatives is "you."

Go to bed.   Do your homework.   Come here.   Sit down.

Be quiet.   Think about it.   Stay there.   Turn it in.

To form a negative imperative, use "don't" and the base form of the verb (no "to").

Don't go to bed.   Don't do your homework.   Don't do that.   Don't come late.

To soften an oral command, you may use the word "please." It sounds a little more polite.

Please do this.   Don't do that, please.

Exercise 6.10   Read all of these instructions before you begin this exercise.

1. Draw a large circle in the middle of this square.

2. In the upper right-hand side of the square, write your name.

3. Under your name, write your father's first name.

4. At the bottom of the square write the name of the nicest person in this class.

5. Above that name, write the name of this textbook.

6. Draw a square around the circle that is in the middle of the square.

7. Inside the circle, draw a tree.

8. After you read all of these instructions, do only number ten.

9. Put your name in the upper left side of this square and sit quietly in your seat until the teacher says to stop.

10. Put your name in the upper left side of this square and sit quietly in your seat until the teacher says to stop.

Exercise 6.11 Write an appropriate command for each of these sentences. Follow the examples.

Examples

Mary closes the door loudly.

Close the door softly, Mary. *or* Don't close the door loudly, Mary.

Mark never comes to class on time.

Come to class on time, Mark. *or* Don't come late to class, Mark.

1. Luanne never pays the rent on time.

2. Jaime spends too much time with her horse.

3. Juan never calls before he comes over to my house.

   _____

4. Henri doesn't take his vitamins.

   _____

5. Kim Lee doesn't indent her paragraphs.

   _____

Exercise 6.12   Rewrite this paragraph. Where logical, change the instructions to commands using the imperative.

   One of my family's favorite vegetables is corn-on-the-cob, and it is easy to make if you follow these steps. First, you put two quarts of cold water on the stove and you turn the burner on high. Next, you add a half teaspoon of salt to the water. When the water is boiling, you put in the corn and you let it cook for five minutes. Then you take the corn out of the water and you serve it hot with butter. My family loves to eat fresh, hot corn-on-the-cob in the summer, and I bet your family will, too!

Exercise 6.13

1. Tell your best friend how to be a successful student in this class. Use commands.

   a. _____

   b. _____

   c. _____

   d. _____

2. Tell your (future?) son or daughter how to be happy in life. Use commands.

   a. _____

   b. _____

   c. _____

   d. _____

3. Tell the leader of your country what to do to improve your country. Use commands.

a. _____

b. _____

c. _____

d. _____

Exercise 6.14 Use one of the three lists from Exercise 6.13 to make a paragraph. Use commands in the paragraph. A possible topic sentence for the first list could be:

> If you would like to become a successful student in this class, just follow these five easy steps.

_____

_____

_____

_____

_____

_____

_____

_____

Exercise 6.15 Share your paragraph with a classmate. Circle all the commands in his/her paragraph. Tell your classmate if you agree or disagree with the advice in his/her paragraph.

MODAL AUXILIARIES

Modal auxiliaries are often found in the secondary support (supporting details) of a process paragraph. They can be used to give options, advice, warnings, or hints about the main steps your paragraph is describing.

We will study two modals that are commonly used to give advice *(should* and *can)* and two modals that express necessity or obligation *(must* and *have to).* First let's look at how the modals are used in sentences, and then we will practice using them in paragraphs.

Placing Modal Auxiliaries in Sentences

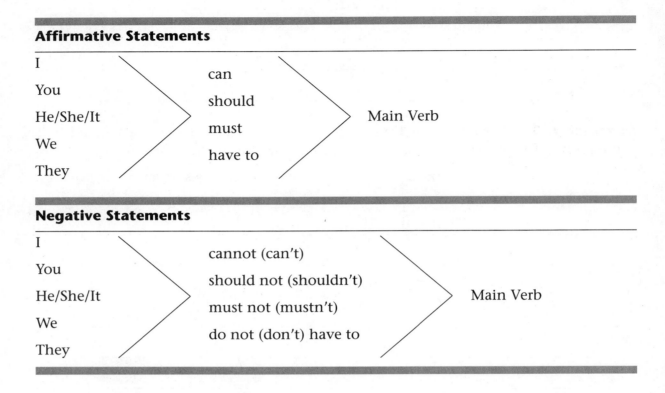

Affirmative Statements

| I You He/She/It We They | can should must have to | Main Verb |

Negative Statements

| I You He/She/It We They | cannot (can't) should not (shouldn't) must not (mustn't) do not (don't) have to | Main Verb |

Understanding and Using Modal Auxiliaries

- ### Can

Can shows ability or possibility.

Examples

> You **can** serve six people with this delicious recipe.
> You **can** complete the job more quickly if you follow these steps.

Exercise 6.16 List five special abilities that you have (craft, hobby, special talent, and so on). Use the modal *can* in each of the sentences.

Example

I **can** cook paella.

1. _____
2. _____
3. _____
4. _____
5. _____

List five abilities that you would like to have but do not. Use *cannot* in each of the sentences.

Examples

I **cannot** speak Chinese (unfortunately).

I **cannot** play the piano (unfortunately).

1. _____
2. _____
3. _____
4. _____
5. _____

Should

Should is used to give advice or suggestions.

Examples

You **should** wait twenty minutes after you eat before swimming.

You **should** not pay for a job until it is finished.

You **should** serve this dish hot.

Exercise 6.17 Read the following situations and use *should* in a sentence offering advice.

1. My tea is cold.

   _____

2. I have a headache.

   _____

3. I lost my pencil.

   _____

4. I don't have my book today.

   _____

5. I lost my job.

   _____

• *Have to* and *must*

Have to and *must* indicate necessity or obligation (when they are used in the affirmative). Notice that *have to* must be conjugated.

Examples

The glue **has to** dry before you move the frame.
The glue **must** dry before you move the frame.

Exercise 6.18 Tell your partner three things that he/she *must* do in order to learn English quickly.

1. _____

2. _____

3. _____

Exercise 6.19 Tell your partner three things that he/she *has to* do in order to be a good citizen in this country.

1. _____

2. _____

3. _____

In the negative form, *have to* and *must* do NOT mean the same thing. "You MUST NOT go" means that it is prohibited or forbidden to go. "You DON'T HAVE TO go" means that it is optional for you to go (you can go if you want to, but it is not necessary.)

Examples

You **do not have to** serve this bean dish with rice. (…but you can if you want.)

You **must not** go through a red light. (…it is against the law!)

Exercise 6.20 Use **must not (mustn't)** or **do not have to (don't have to)** to create sentences with these phrases. Make sure your sentences are logical.

1. Go 100 miles per hour on a freeway

   _____

2. Watch television in the evening

   _____

3. Steal from stores

   _____

4. Learn German if you live in France

   _____

5. Go outside during a hurricane

   _____

Exercise 6.21   Select two of the five abilities you listed in Exercise 6.16 that require a series of steps to accomplish and that you would like to write about. Consider how many steps the process involves, the vocabulary it will take to describe each step, and the interest you think the class and teacher will have in reading about your process (in other words, consider your audience!). Write these two topics here.

1. _____

2. _____

Ask five of your classmates which of these two topics sounds the most interesting to them and mark the results here by checking off a box for each vote.

Topic #1 votes   **Topic #2 votes**

❏   ❏

❏   ❏

❏   ❏

❏   ❏

❏   ❏

The most popular topic will be a topic for a paragraph. Develop a list of all the steps involved in the process. When you have finished, check to see that your list is complete, that it covers all the steps in the process, and that it is in chronological order.

Next, sit with a partner (or in small groups), and explain the steps in your process to him/her (or the group). Answer any questions your classmate(s) might have about the process, and add those details to your list. When you finish, listen to your classmate(s)' process. Point out anything that is not clear about it. Ask questions about any vocabulary you do not understand.

Write a paragraph of process using the details from the list you developed above.

_____

_____

_____

_____

_____

Write a paragraph of process about one of the processes your classmates explained to you.

_____

_____

_____

_____

_____

_____

Write paragraphs for each of the two lists you developed on page 143 (registering for classes and buying books at a bookstore).

_____

_____

_____

_____

_____

_____

VOCABULARY BUILDING

Write ten new vocabulary words that you learned in class this week. Next to each word, write the translation for the word in your own language. Then write the word in a sentence.

1. _____

   _____

2. _____

   _____

3. _____

   _____

4. _____

_____

5. _____

_____

6. _____

_____

7. _____

_____

8. _____

_____

9. _____

_____

10. _____

_____

CLASSROOM FEEDBACK

1. Tell your teacher how to improve this class. Use commands.

   Example Please speak more slowly in class. Sometimes I do not understand you.

   a. _____

   b. _____

   c. _____

2. Tell your teacher what NOT to change. Use negative commands.

   Example Please don't change handouts you give because they help me learn.

   a. _____

   b. _____

   c. _____

chapter
seven

Process Paragraphs—Part 2

Remember the five steps for writing a process paragraph from Chapter 6:

■ STEP ONE
Write the topic sentence.

■ STEP TWO
List the support for your topic sentence.

■ STEP THREE
Put the supporting sentences in chronological order.

■ STEP FOUR
Connect the supporting sentences with connecting words.

■ STEP FIVE
Write the conclusion.

The computer programs that accompany this section are called: "Connecting Words" and "Connecting Words Test" (Macintosh and IBM)

CONNECTING SENTENCES IN PROCESS PARAGRAPHS

Subordinating conjunctions of time (*when, while, as soon as, as, before, after,* etc.) and transition words (*first, afterwards, then, after that, lastly, finally,* etc.) connect the supporting sentences in the body of your paragraph and help your reader understand the chronological order of the actions you are describing. Using these words to connect sentences can make your paragraph sound fluent. Notice the difference between the two paragraphs below. The first uses very few subordinating conjunctions or sentence connectors. It doesn't sound fluent. Notice how the second paragraph uses a variety of sentence connectors and sentence structures.

Exercise 7.1 In the next two paragraphs, underline all of the connecting words.

1. How to Write a Descriptive Paragraph

Writing a paragraph of description is easy if you follow these steps. Develop a topic sentence. Find a topic. Focus it. Brainstorm to find a controlling idea. Write the focused topic and the controlling idea in a complete sentence. Develop the support for your topic sentence. Describe three aspects of your focused topic in this support. All of the support will develop the controlling idea. Connect the details that develop the controlling idea to the aspect that you are describing with coordinating conjunctions and transition words. Develop the conclusion. It may be your opinion about the topic. It may be a restatement of the topic sentence using other words. It is easy to write a paragraph of description.

2. How to Write a Descriptive Paragraph

Writing a descriptive paragraph is easy if you follow these steps. First, you need to develop your topic sentence. To do this, you must find a topic and focus it. As soon as you focus your topic, you are ready to think of a controlling idea. After you have your controlling idea, combine the focused topic and the controlling idea, and write them in one complete sentence. This is your topic sentence. In the next part of your descriptive paragraph, you need to write three supporting ideas. These supporting ideas will describe three different aspects of your focused topic while they develop the controlling idea. As soon as you plan your supporting ideas and organize them logically, you need to write them in complete sentences. As you write, you should connect some of the sentences in your paragraph with coordinating conjunctions, subordinators, and transition words. Finally, you are ready to write the conclusion. The conclusion may be your opinion about the topic, a restatement of the topic sentence, or a summary of the paragraph. Writing a descriptive paragraph is not difficult, and if you plan it well before you write, you will do a good job.

Discuss with a partner: How does the second paragraph above sound different from the first? Why?

Exercise 7.2 Do this exercise with a partner or in small groups. Plan and write a paragraph of process. The topic is "How to Study for a Test."

Subordinating Conjunctions

• *When*

> When I want to relax, I read a book in the park.

When you use *when* as a subordinator, the action that is described in the dependent clause (the *when* clause) happens first or at the same time as the action in the other part of the sentence (the independent clause). *When* can also mean "every time." **Do not use the future tense in the subordinate (dependent) clause.**

Examples

> When you enter the store $\boxed{,}$ you see shelves everywhere.
> **TWO MEANINGS:** FIRST YOU ENTER THE STORE; THEN YOU SEE THE SHELVES.
> EVERY TIME YOU WALK IN, YOU SEE THE SHELVES.

> Ana María always looks out for children on the road when she drives.
> **ONE MEANING:** EVERY TIME SHE DRIVES, SHE LOOKS OUT FOR CHILDREN.

Exercise 7.3 Look at the following schedule, and then write "T" or "F" in the blank to indicate if the sentence is true or false according to the information in the schedule.

Schedule

8:20	Teacher arrives at class.
8:40	Students arrive at class.
8:50	Students take a test.
9:30	Students leave the classroom.

T / F

___ 1. When the students arrive at class, the teacher is there.

___ 2. When the teacher arrives at class, the students are there.

___ 3. When the students take a test, they leave the classroom.

___ 4. When the students finish a test, they leave the classroom.

• *While*[1] as a Subordinator of Time

> We should go to the beach while the sun is shining.

When you use *while,* the actions in the sentence are happening at the same time. As you can see in the following examples, the verb in the *while* clause can be in the present continuous tense (first example) if the action in the main clause is occurring now or in the simple present tense (second example) if the action in the main clause happens habitually. It is also common to use the simple present tense after *while* to indicate actions that happen at the same time IF the verb in the main clause is in the future tense. **Do not use the future tense in the *while* clause.**

Examples

While you are studying $\boxed{,}$ I am typing the papers. **(now)**
(WE ARE BOTH DOING THESE ACTIONS NOW.)

While Ana María drives $\boxed{,}$ she looks out for children on the road.
(EVERY TIME THAT SHE DRIVES, SHE ALSO LOOKS OUT FOR CHILDREN.)

While you study $\boxed{,}$ I will type the papers. **(later)**
(WE WILL BOTH BE DOING THESE ACTIONS AT THE SAME TIME.)

Do NOT use both *when* and *while* in the same sentence. Look at the following examples.

wrong: **While** I was sleeping **when** the baby cried.

correct: I was sleeping **when** the baby cried.

When the baby cried $\boxed{,}$ I was sleeping.

The baby cried **while** I was sleeping.

While I was sleeping $\boxed{,}$ the baby cried.

Exercise 7.4 Look around the class, and make a list of the activities of five of your classmates or teacher using *while.*

Example

While my teacher is writing on the board, Jorge is writing in his notebook and looking at the board.

1. _____

2. _____

---

1 *While* can also indicate a contrast (e.g., While he probably won't enjoy the movie, he will appreciate the actors). In that case, the future tense is possible, AND a comma is acceptable even when the subordinate clause is not at the beginning of the sentence. Here, we are studying *while* only as it is used to show simultaneous action.

3. _____

4. _____

5. _____

Exercise 7.5 With a partner, combine these sentences using *while*.

1. You will write the answers to Chapter 1. / I will write the answers to Chapter 2.

   _____

2. It is raining. / We are staying in the house.

   _____

3. The baby is sleeping. / Tom will study his math.

   _____

4. The baby is sleeping. / I need to wash the dishes.

   _____

5. The cake is baking. / Make the frosting.

   _____

Exercise 7.6 With a partner, circle the error(s) in these sentences and rewrite each sentence correctly.

1. While you sleep, when I finished painting the bathroom.

   _____

2. When you will go to the bank, please cash this check for me.

   _____

3. I need to buy some clothes while I go downtown this afternoon.

   _____

4. When you have finished with that exercise do this one.

   _____

5. While you are learning to write English you are also learning to speak it.

   _____

● *As soon as*

As soon as you close the door, I will turn on the air conditioner.

When you use *as soon as,* the action that is described in the dependent clause happens just before another action occurs. You may NOT use the future tense (or the present continuous tense) in clauses that begin with *as soon as.*

Examples

As soon as you finish $\boxed{,}$ we are going to leave.
(FIRST YOU WILL FINISH. THEN WE WILL LEAVE.)

Put in the spaghetti **as soon as** the water begins to boil.
(FIRST THE WATER BEGINS TO BOIL. THEN YOU PUT IN THE SPAGHETTI.)

Exercise 7.7 Rewrite these sentences using *as soon as.* Make sure the sentences keep the same meaning.

1. First, the dryer will stop; then you will take out the clothes and fold them.

   _____

2. First, you focus the camera. Then you take the picture.

   _____

3. First, put the oil in the pan. Then turn on the burner.

   _____

4. First, turn on the computer. Next, put in the disk.

   _____

● **After**

illogical: I put on the parachute **after** I jumped out of the plane. **(You would probably die!)**
(THIS MEANS THAT FIRST YOU JUMPED OUT OF THE PLANE; THEN YOU PUT ON THE PARACHUTE!)

logical: I jumped out of the plane **after** I put on the parachute.

   or **After** I put on the parachute $\boxed{,}$ I jumped out of the plane.

Remember that when you use *after,* the action that follows *after* (in the subordinate, or dependent, clause) occurs first. The action in the independent clause happens second. **Do not use the future tense in the *after* clause.**

Exercise 7.8 Rewrite these sentences using *after*. Make sure the sentences keep the same meaning.

1. First, wash your hands with antibacterial soap. Next, put on the surgical gloves.

   _____

2. First, you will close the door. Second, you will lock the door and turn on the alarm.

   _____

3. First, focus the topic. Then decide on a controlling idea.

   _____

4. First, you brainstorm and make a concept map. Then you write your paragraph.

   _____

5. First, put the filter in the pot. Afterwards, pour coffee into the filter.

   _____

• *Before*

You should count to ten before you say anything when you are angry.

The action that follows *before* (in the subordinate clause) is the action that occurs SECOND or last. The action in the independent clause happens first. Remember—you may NOT use the future tense in the *before* clause.

    wrong: **Before** we will go to the lab, we will finish this class.

    correct: **Before** we go to the lab, we will finish this class.

Exercise 7.9 Look at the schedule below and tell if the sentences on the following pages are logical (L) or illogical (I).

    7:50 Pierre goes into the movie theater.
    7:52 Janine goes into the movie theater.
    8:00 The movie starts.
    8:30 Pierre goes out to buy popcorn.
    8:33 Janine goes out to buy a soda.
    8:35 Pierre meets Janine in the lobby.
    8:40 Pierre and Janine return to the movie together.

L / I

___ 1. Janine goes out to buy a soda before Pierre goes out to buy popcorn.

___ 2. After Pierre goes out to buy popcorn, the movie starts.

___ 3. Janine goes into the movie theater before Pierre arrives.

___ 4. Pierre and Janine return to the movie together before they buy popcorn and soda.

___ 5. Before Janine goes out to buy soda, Pierre goes out to buy popcorn.

Exercise 7.10 Combine the following sentences two different ways using *before* or *after*.

Example

(before) First, we took the test. / Then we went to the cafeteria.

    a. Before we went to the cafeteria, we took the test.

    b. We took the test before we went to the cafeteria.

1. (after) First, I went to the bank. / Then I went to the store.

    a. After _____ , _____ .

    b. _____ after _____ .

2. (after) First, he graduated. / Then he got a good job.

    a. After _____ , _____ .

    b. _____ after _____ .

3. (before) First, we filled out the papers for our insurance. / Then we began to work on our roof.

    a. Before _____ , _____ .

    b. _____ before _____ .

4. (before) First, we heard a loud explosion. / Then we saw fire coming from the building.

    a. Before _____ , _____ .

    b. _____ before _____ .

Exercise 7.11 Fill in the blanks with punctuation (commas) and/or *after, before, when, if.*

The students in the International Students Program at the Kendall campus of Miami-Dade Community College have their own private laboratory with two modern computer labs (1) _____ a language lab (2) _____ and a place where they can go to practice computerized lessons between their classes. To use the computer lab (3) _____ students go to room 6237 and fill out a small white card with the name of the computer program they want to use. (4) _____ the students are ready to begin the program (5) _____ they must first show a class schedule to the lab attendant and give the attendant the white card with the name of the program. (6) _____ they show the attendant the schedule (7) _____ the attendant gives each student a computer disk (8) _____ and the students are ready to do lessons on the Apple computer. The students go into the Apple lab (9) _____ find an empty seat (10) _____ turn on the computer (11) _____ and insert the disk. (12) _____ the students finish the lesson (13) _____ they can go into the main part of the lab and get help from the professor who is there to tutor them. (14) _____ the students leave the lab (15) _____ they need to return the computer disk to the attendants (16) _____ and the attendants will give each student a card that shows how much time he/she was on the computer (17) _____ what lesson the student did (18) _____ and what class the student is in. The international students feel comfortable in this modern lab.

Exercise 7.12 Go with a classmate to a lab or a library on your campus. Plan and write a process paragraph with your classmate. You can use the paragraph above as a model.

_____

_____

_____

_____

Exercise 7.13 Use coordinating conjunctions *(and, but, so)*, subordinators *(because, after, if)*, and transitional words and expressions *(first, next, afterwards, then, finally)* to combine these sentences.

1. I have a headache. / I went to bed late last night and woke up too early this morning.

   _____

2. It might rain tomorrow. / I won't go to the park with John.

   _____

3. Oneida studies in the library every week. / She stays for several hours.

   _____

4. You came late to class. / You missed the test.

   _____

5. You will come late to class tomorrow. / You will miss the test.

   _____

6. First we will drive to the store. /   Then we will go to the bank.

   _____

7. First we ate dinner. / Then we washed the dishes.

   _____

Transitional Words and Expressions

The following transitional words and expressions are used to introduce the separate steps in a paragraph of process:

USE OF TRANSITIONAL WORDS AND PHRASES IN PROCESS PARAGRAPHS

Word or Phrase	Common Use
first *first of all* *second*	For the first step in the process.
also *in addition*	To add extra information to any step.
afterwards *after that* *then* *next*	For any step in the process EXCEPT the first.
during this time *meanwhile* *at the same time*	For a second SIMULTANEOUS action.
finally *lastly*	For the last step in the support.
in conclusion	Sometimes used for a conclusion, but only if the paragraph is quite long. It is not common in process paragaphs.

Use these transition words to introduce the main supporting sentences in a paragraph of process, in other words, to introduce the steps. The patterns of punctuation for transition words were presented in a previous chapter:

First sentence [;] transition word [,] second sentence.
First sentence [.] Transition word [,] second sentence.
First sentence [.] Subject (be) [,] short transition word [,] rest of sentence.

You put the tape into the recorder and press the rewind button [;] **afterwards** [,] **you** press *play.*

You put the tape into the recorder and press the rewind button [.] **After that** [,] **you** press *play.*

You put the tape into the recorder and press the rewind button [.] **You then** press *play.*

● *First, First of all*

> It is easy to bake a chocolate cake. First of all, you need to gather the ingredients.

The words *first* and *first of all* can be used to introduce the first step in a paragraph of process. They are transitional expressions and follow the same punctuation patterns as transition words, except that if you use *first* after a subject, commas are not necessary.

Examples

> It is easy to bake a chocolate cake. **First** $\boxed{,}$ you need to gather the ingredients.

> It is easy to bake a chocolate cake. You **first** need to gather the ingredients.

When you use transition words to introduce the main steps in your process paragraph, do not use semicolons for the punctuation. Use periods. The main steps are separate supporting ideas and should not be connected to any preceding sentence as you develop the body.

> **wrong:** It is easy to bake a chocolate cake $\boxed{;}$ **First,** you need to gather the ingredients.

> **correct:** It is easy to bake a chocolate cake $\boxed{.}$ **First,** you need to gather the ingredients.

Exercise 7.14 Fill in the blanks three different ways with correct punctuation and the transition words *first* and *first of all*.

1. A popular breakfast dish in the United States is called French toast, and it is relatively easy to cook _____ you need to put four pieces of bread, two eggs, half a cup of milk, vanilla, and cinnamon on the counter.

2. A popular breakfast dish in the United States is called French toast, and it is relatively easy to cook _____ you need to put four pieces of bread, two eggs, half a cup of milk, vanilla, and cinnamon on the counter.

3. A popular breakfast dish in the United States is called French toast, and it is relatively easy to cook. You _____ need to put four pieces of bread, two eggs, half a cup of milk, vanilla, and cinnamon on the counter.

(You did not use semicolons in the above sentences, did you?)

- ## *In addition, also*

There are many fish at the Seaquarium $\boxed{.}$ **In addition** $\boxed{,}$ there are two great white sharks.

There are many fish at the Seaquarium $\boxed{;}$ **in addition** $\boxed{,}$ there are two great white sharks.

There are many fish at the Seaquarium $\boxed{.}$ **There are** $\boxed{,}$ **in addition** $\boxed{,}$ two great white sharks.

There are many fish at the Seaquarium $\boxed{.}$ **Also** $\boxed{,}$ there are two great white sharks.

There are many fish at the Seaquarium $\boxed{;}$ **also** $\boxed{,}$ there are two great white sharks.

There are many fish at the Seaquarium $\boxed{.}$ **There are also** two great white sharks.

The words *in addition* and *also* can be used to give extra details to a main supporting idea (or step) in a paragraph of process. They are transitional expressions and follow the same punctuation patterns as transition words, except that if you use *also* (or any other transition word of four letters or fewer) after a subject, commas are not necessary. See Chapter 3 for more explanation and exercises on these two transition words.

Exercise 7.15 Combine each pair of sentences into a single sentence using the transition word in parentheses. Be sure to use correct punctuation.

1. Sharks are dangerous when they are hungry. They are dangerous when they feel threatened. (in addition)

   _____

   _____

2. Sharks are dangerous when they are hungry. They are dangerous when they feel threatened. (In addition)

   _____

   _____

3. Sharks are dangerous when they are hungry. They are dangerous when they feel threatened. (Also)

   _____

   _____

4. Sharks are dangerous when they are hungry. They are dangerous when they feel threatened. (also)

   _____

   _____

● *Afterwards, then, after that, next*

To plant a small garden with carrots and radishes is not too difficult if you follow these steps. First, spade the soil of your garden with a shovel. **After that,** remove the weeds, and break the clods of dirt into fine granules with a hoe or a rake. **Next,** make four straight furrows and water them. Then plant the carrot seeds in two of the furrows and the radish seeds in the other two furrows. Cover each seed with dirt and tamp the soil. **Afterwards,** put a stick at the head of each row, and attach the seed packet to the stick, so you can identify what you have planted in each row. It is not easy to plant a garden, but the exercise is wonderful for your body, and the food you grow will help your budget!

These transition words can be used to introduce the second, third, fourth (etc.) steps in a paragraph of process. All of these words except *then* follow the normal rules of punctuation for transition words. Just like all transition words that have four letters or fewer, the transition *then* does not need commas when it is inside of a clause. *Then* also does **not** need a comma after it when it is at the beginning of a clause.

Examples

As soon as you dial the number, deposit the money $\boxed{.}$ **After that** $\boxed{,}$ the operator will ask you for your name.

As soon as you dial the number, deposit the money $\boxed{;}$ **after that** $\boxed{,}$ the operator will ask you for your name.

As soon as you dial the number, deposit the money $\boxed{.}$ **Afterwards** $\boxed{,}$ the operator will ask you for your name.

As soon as you dial the number, deposit the money $\boxed{;}$ **afterwards** $\boxed{,}$ the operator will ask you for your name.

As soon as you dial the number, deposit the money $\boxed{.}$ **Then** the operator will ask you for your name.

As soon as you dial the number, deposit the money $\boxed{;}$ **then** the operator will ask you for your name.

As soon as you dial the number, deposit the money $\boxed{.}$ The operator will **then** ask you for your name.

Exercise 7.16 Connect these two sentences using the expressions in parentheses. Don't use *first* or *second* in your sentences.

First, cash the check at the bank.

Second, buy a money order.

1. (then) _____

_____

2. (afterwards) _____

_____

3. (next) _____

_____

4. (after that) _____

_____

● *Meanwhile, in the meantime, at the same time*

   Everyone in John's family helps out around the house, and tonight is no exception. John is washing the dishes. **Meanwhile,** his wife is clearing off the table. **At the same time,** his son is vacuuming the living room, and his daughter is putting away the magazines and newspapers. The family is working hard together cleaning up after dinner. It is easy to see why everyone in John's family is happy. They are a team.

These transition words are used to introduce an action that happens at the same time as the action in the previous sentence.

Exercise 7.17 Write original sentences using the following words.

1. meanwhile

_____

2. at the same time

_____

3. in the meantime

_____

● *Finally, lastly, in conclusion*

Taking your baby for a walk in the park can be a wonderful way for you to spend the afternoon, and if you prepare adequately for the trip, you will be sure to have a relaxing time. Before you leave the house, there are several items that you should pack. You should take a bottle of milk, water, or juice in case your baby gets thirsty. As you are preparing the bottle, you might consider putting some cookies or a banana in the bag in case the baby gets hungry while you are at the park. After you have prepared the food, you should put a few diapers and a blanket or jacket in the stroller. **Finally,** you are ready to dress your baby warmly and head to the park. **(In conclusion,)** if you prepare well before you leave your house, you will be ready for any emergency that might arise.

Use the transition words *finally* and *lastly* to introduce the last step in a process paragraph (not for the conclusion). The expression *in conclusion* is commonly used for longer paragraphs. In short paragraphs, more common concluding sentences for a paragraph of process include invitations for the reader to try the process you have described or a general statement about the topic.

Exercise 7.18 Do this exercise with a partner. Use *lastly* or *finally* to connect each group of sentences. Then add a conclusion.

Example

Put the roses in the vase, and fill the vase with cool water. / Put an aspirin in the water to keep the flowers fresh, and put the vase on the table.

Put the roses in the vase, and fill the vase with cool water. Lastly, put an aspirin in the water to keep the flowers fresh, and put the vase on the table. If you follow these steps carefully, you will make a beautiful centerpiece for your dinner table.

1. Now remove the cake from the oven, let it sit for fifteen minutes, and frost it. / Cut the cake into triangular pieces, and serve it warm with a glass of cold milk.

   _____

   _____

   _____

2. Allow the raw fish to marinate for one hour in the lemon juice and onions. / Serve it with white rice.

_____

_____

_____

3. Remove the disk from the computer, and select "Shut down" from the "Special" menu. / Reach behind the computer and press the "off" switch.

_____

_____

_____

Exercise 7.19 To review all connecting words, do this exercise with a partner. Use coordinating conjunctions (*and, but, so, yet,* etc.), subordinators (*because, after, if,* etc.), or transition words (*afterwards, therefore, first of all,* etc.) to combine these groups of sentences. Use the most logical connecting word. Replace repeated nouns with pronouns.

1. The baby is crying. / The baby is not sick. / The baby might be sleepy. / The baby might be hungry. / The baby might be hot.

_____

_____

2. Mark graduated from college. / Steve graduated from college. / Mary graduated from college. / None of them can find a good job. / They are depressed.

_____

_____

3. Marsha bought some new eyeglasses. / They don't help her see very well. / I think she needs a new eye doctor.

_____

_____

4. You turned on the computer. / You opened the program. / You selected the correct lesson for the day. / You finished the lesson. / You took the computer test. / You told the teacher your grade. / You turned off the computer.

_____

_____

5. I drink some coffee. (simultaneously) I prepare their school lunches. / We finish breakfast. / The children and I get into the car. / We drive to school. / I leave them at their school. / I go to work.

_____

_____

Exercise 7.20 Focus one of the following topics, and then plan and write a process paragraph about it.

    hobbies   crafts   special skills   recipes   sports

_____

_____

_____

_____

_____

VOCABULARY BUILDING

Write ten new vocabulary words that you learned in class this week. Next to each word, write the translation for the word in your own language. Then write the word in a sentence.

1. _____

   _____

2. _____

   _____

3. _____

   _____

4. _____

_____

5. _____

_____

6. _____

_____

7. _____

_____

8. _____

_____

9. _____

_____

10. _____

_____

TEACHER FEEDBACK

Write for ten minutes without stopping. Answer this question: What have you learned in this class?

appendix one

The Present and Present Continuous Tenses

In this appendix, you can review the basic rules for writing the simple present and the present continuous tenses of verbs. You need to use these two tenses to write paragraphs of description and process.

 The computer program that accompanies this section is called: "Present and Present Continuous" (Macintosh and IBM)

Simple Present Tense of *be*

STATEMENT	I am (I'm)...	He is ('s)...	We are ('re)...
		She is ('s)...	You are ('re)...
		It is ('s)...	They are ('re)...
NEGATIVE	I am not (I'm not)...	He is not ('s not)(isn't)...	We are not ('re not)(aren't)...
		She is not ('s not)(isn't)...	You are not ('re not)(aren't)...
		It is not ('s not)(isn't)...	They are not ('re not)(aren't)...
QUESTION	Am I...	Is he...	Are we...
		Is she...	Are you...
		Is it...	Are they...
NEGATIVE QUESTION	Aren't I...	Isn't he...	Aren't we...
		Isn't she...	Aren't you...
		Isn't it...	Aren't they...
SHORT ANSWER (AFFIRM.)	Yes, I am.	Yes, he is.	Yes, we are.
		Yes, she is.	Yes, you are.
		Yes, it is.	Yes, they are.

Simple Present Tense of *be* (cont.)

SHORT ANSWER (NEG.)	No, I'm not.	No, he's not (he isn't).	No, we're not (we aren't).
		No, she's not (she isn't).	No, you're not (you aren't).
		No, it's not (it isn't).	No, they're not (they aren't).

SIMPLE PRESENT TENSE

BE

● Affirmative form

Be has three forms in the affirmative: *am, is,* and *are* (see chart above).

● Negative form

There is only one contraction form for *I.* (*Am + not* is never contracted.[1])

● Affirmative questions

To make questions with "be," don't use an auxiliary (no *do* or *does*). Put *is, am,* or *are* in front of the subject.

● Negative questions

Use the contracted forms of *be + not* to make negative questions, even in academic paragraphs.

● Short answers

You can use short answers in speaking, but they are not commonly used in formal academic writing. In a conversation, you use short answers to respond to a question in a brief way. You should never contract (use an apostrophe with) the affirmative short answer. You should always contract the negative short answer unless you want to sound emphatic.

---

1 In very informal (colloquial) speech, you will hear *ain't* as a contraction for *am + not,* but it is **not** correct and should be avoided.

PRESENT TENSE REGULAR VERBS

Simple Present Tense of Regular Verbs (not *be*)

STATEMENT	I… you… we… they…	He… She… It…
NEGATIVE	I don't… you don't… we don't… they don't…	He doesn't… She doesn't… It doesn't…
QUESTION	Do I… Do you… Do we… Do they…	Does he… Does she… Does it…
NEGATIVE QUESTION	Don't I… Don't you… Don't we… Don't they…	Doesn't he… Doesn't she … Doesn't it…
SHORT ANSWER (AFFIRM.)	Yes, I do. Yes, you do. Yes, we do. Yes, they do.	Yes, he does. Yes, she does. Yes, it does.
SHORT ANSWER (NEG.)	No, I don't. No, you don't. No, we don't. No, they don't.	No, he doesn't. No, she doesn't. No, it doesn't.

• Affirmative

When forming the present tense of regular verbs, the third person singular always ends in *-s.* *Somebody, nobody, someone,* and *no one* are also singular pronouns.

• Negative

When you use regular verbs in the negative form, use *does not* or *do not* or the contractions *doesn't/don't* (in informal writing). The main verb does NOT take an *-s* in the negative.

• Affirmative questions

For regular verbs in the question form, use the auxiliary *do* or *does.* The main verb does NOT take an *-s* in questions.

• Negative questions

Just like with the verb *be,* you may use the contracted forms of *do/does + not* to make negative questions, even in academic writing. Notice that the third person uses "doesn't."

• Short answers

Short answers are used in speaking; not in formal academic writing. They are used to answer a question in a brief way. The affirmative short answer is never contracted. The negative short answer is usually contracted, unless you want to sound emphatic.

PRESENT CONTINUOUS (PROGRESSIVE)

Present Continuous (or Progressive) Tense of *to go*		
STATEMENT	I am going.	He is going.
	You are going.	She is going.
	We are going.	It is going.
	They are going.	

NEGATIVE	I am not going.	He is not (isn't) going.
	You are not (aren't) going.	She is not (isn't) going.
	We are not (aren't) going.	It is not (isn't) going.
	They are not (aren't) going.	
QUESTION	Am I going?	Is he going?
	Are you going?	Is she going?
	Are we going?	Is it going?
	Are they going?	
NEGATIVE QUESTION	Aren't I going?	Isn't he going?
	Aren't you going?	Isn't she going?
	Aren't we going?	Isn't it going?
	Aren't they going?	
SHORT ANSWER (AFFIRM.)	Yes, I am.	Yes, he is.
	Yes, you are	Yes, she is.
	Yes, we are.	Yes, it is.
	Yes, they are.	
SHORT ANSWER (NEG.)	No, I am not (I'm not).	No, he is not (isn't).
	No, you are not (you're not).	No, she is not (isn't).
	No, we are not (we're not).	No, it is not (isn't).
	No, they are not (they're not).	

● Spelling rules for present participles

1. For words that end in consonant + *e,* drop the *-e* and add *-ing.* (believe = believing)

2. When the verb ends in *consonant + vowel + consonant* and has the stress on the last syllable, you must double the final consonant. (occúr = occúrring) The two exceptions to this rule are words that end in *W* and *X* (sew = sewing, box = boxing)

3. For verbs that end in two consonants or *-Y,* just add *-ing* (bless = blessing, reply = replying)

4. For verbs that end in *-ie,* change the *-ie* to *-y* and add *-ing.* (die = dying)

● Affirmative

For the present continuous tense of regular verbs, use the verb *be* and put *-ing* on the main verb (making it a present participle).

● Negative

For the negative form of the present continuous, use the negative auxiliaries *am/is/are* + not, and the verb with *-ing*.

● Affirmative questions

When using the present continuous in the question form, use the auxiliary *be*. The main verb needs *-ing*.

● Negative questions

Use the contracted forms of *is/are* + *not* to make negative questions, even in academic writing. Notice (chart above) that the main verb always requires *-ing* with the present continuous. The form for *I* in negative questions is *Aren't I* + verb-*ing*. This is because there is no grammatically correct contraction for *am* + *not*.

USE OF THE PRESENT CONTINUOUS AND SIMPLE PRESENT TENSES[2]

The Present Continuous (Progressive) Tense

The present continuous tense is used for three different kinds of actions:

1. Actions that are in progress at this moment.
   It **is raining.** / The dogs **are barking.**

2. Future action IF the sentence also has an adverb of time such as *tomorrow* or *later*.
   Hans **is coming** over **later.** / I **am doing** it **tomorrow.**

3. To express a habitual action that annoys or bothers you.
   My teacher **is always forgetting** my name. / He **is always coming** late to class.

---

2 For extensive drill and practice on this, do the accompanying computer program called Present/Continuous.

Example

My friend, Martha **is always doing** odd things. For example, she **is always offering** to give us a ride home even though she doesn't have a car. Furthermore, she **is always carrying** her pet cat, Simon, on her head and **pretending** that it is a new style of hat. Sometimes, when you go to her house in the afternoon, you can see her painting with her toes on the patio. I know my friend is weird, but I like her because she **is always surprising and entertaining me** with her strange behavior.

The Simple Present Tense

The simple present tense is used to talk about:

1. General statements of fact or daily habits, activities, and repeated actions.

   I go to the beach on Sundays. / All horses have manes. / It rains in July.

2. Nonaction verbs.
   Even when these verbs are happening in the present moment, they are written with simple present tense (mental states, emotional states, possession, sensory perception, and other existing states).

Nonaction Verbs

Mental States			
know	believe	imagine	want
realize	feel	doubt	need
understand	suppose	remember	mean
prefer	recognize	think	

Emotional States			
love	hate	fear	mind
like	dislike	envy	care

Possession			
possess	have	own	belong

Sensory Perception			
taste	hear	see	smell	feel

Other Existing States				
seem	exist	be	cost	consist of
look	owe	contain	include	appear

Asking Questions

Questions about actions in the present tense are usually made with the words *ever* or *how often.*

> Do you **ever** go to the beach on the weekends?
>
> **How often** do you travel to Spain?
>
> Does your sister **ever** watch television in English?

Adverbs of frequency are common with the present tense. See Chapter 4.

Verbs that Change Meaning According to Tense

Some nonprogressive verbs have continuous forms, but they have different meanings in the continuous and simple present tenses.

think	have	taste	smell	see	feel	look	appear	be

Examples   Study the following sentences.

1. I **think** you are nice. (opinion)
   I **am thinking** about that problem. (action)
2. She **feels** sick. (health)
   She **is feeling** the cat's fur. (action)
3. I **have** a new car. (possession)
   I **am having** a good time. I **am having** lunch. I **am having** a baby. (actions)
4. You **look** beautiful. (perception)
   I **am looking** for my keys. (action)
5. This soup **tastes** wonderful. (perception)
   The cook **is tasting** the soup. (action)
6. You **appear** to be ill. (perception)
   He **is appearing** on stage in Reno. (action)
7. This soup **smells** great! (perception)
   Look at John. He **is smelling** the roses. (action)
8. He **weighs** too much. (existing state)
   He **is weighing** the meat. (action)
9. I **see** the car. (perception)
   I **am seeing** a doctor. (visiting). I **am seeing** John. (dating)
10. He **is** a nice person. (existing state)
    He **is being** nice. (action = behaving)

appendix two

Topic Sentence Don't's

Don't #1: Don't write a fragment as a topic sentence.

The topic sentence must have a complete subject and verb.

Examples of "Don't"

1. My mother's beautiful smile. **(This sentence has no conjugated verb.)**

2. Going to the beach on the weekend with friends. **(This sentence has no conjugated verb.)**

3. When you need to register for classes at UCD. **(This sentence has no independent clause.)**

Corrections

1. My mother has an angelic smile.

2. Going to the beach on the weekend with friends can be fun.

3. Students who register early for classes at UCD have three advantages.

Exercise A2.1 Write your own ORIGINAL corrections for these three examples:

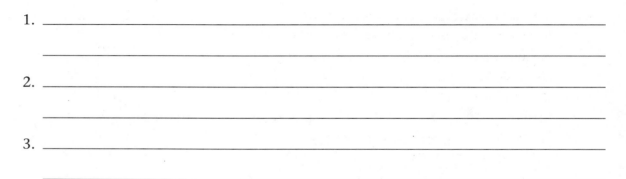

1. _____

   _____

2. _____

   _____

3. _____

   _____

Don't #2: Don't announce the topic.

You should not write expressions like "This paragraph will discuss..." or "I am going to describe..." in your topic sentence. The topic sentence needs to say something interesting and meaningful about the topic to catch the reader's attention. Topic sentences which only announce the topic sound dry and boring and sometimes cause the writer to omit the controlling idea.

Examples of "Don't"

1. **I'm going to tell you about** my mother's smile. **(Readers have no idea what the writer is going to say about the smile because this sentence has no controlling idea.)**

2. **This paragraph will discuss** going to the beach on the weekends with friends. **(Readers have no idea what the paragraph will say about "going to the beach" because there is no controlling idea in this topic sentence.)**

3. **Let me explain about** registering early for classes at this college. **(Again, this sentence has no controlling idea. The readers cannot see what the paragraph will say about registering early. How to do it? Why do it?)**

Corrections

1. This paragraph will discuss the death penalty.

   Anyone convicted of selling dangerous drugs to children should receive the death penalty.

2. I am going to describe my grandmother in this paragraph.

   My grandmother was the most eccentric member of my family.

3. Let me explain about registering early for classes.

   It is easy to register early for classes if you follow these simple steps.

Exercise A2.2 Write your own ORIGINAL corrections for the three following examples:

1. I'm going to tell you about my mother's smile.

   _____

2. This paragraph will discuss going to the beach on the weekends with friends.

   _____

3. Let me explain about registering early for classes at this college.

_____

Don't #3: Don't state the topic sentence as a personal opinion (no "I").

When you write the words, "In my opinion" or "I believe" in your topic sentence, you weaken it. First of all, academic paragraphs should be written objectively. When you sound as if you are offering your personal opinion, your reader may feel free to disagree with you. It is true that the topic sentence usually DOES GIVE your opinion about a person, place, thing, or idea (the controlling idea does this), but you should always write the topic sentence as an objective fact. Stating your opinion in this way (strongly) will make your opinion sound more believable.

Examples of "Don't"

1. **I believe** that my mother's smile is beautiful. **(The topic sentence sounds weak.)**

2. **In my opinion,** going to the beach on the weekend with friends is fun. **(You invite your readers to give their own opinion of what is fun.)**

3. When you need to register for classes at UCD, **I think** you should register early. **(You do not sound like you are sure about what you are saying.)**

More Examples and Their Corrections

1. I **think that** the air pollution in Denver is slowly killing the citizens of that beautiful city.

1. ~~I think that~~ The air pollution in Denver is slowly killing the citizens of that beautiful city.

2. **In my opinion,** grades should be abolished in ESOL and foreign language classes.

2. ~~In my opinion,~~ Grades should be abolished in ESOL and foreign language classes.

3. **I believe that** all houses in Miami should have hurricane shutters.

Exercise A2.3 Correct the third example (above) yourself:

3. _____

Don't #4: Don't include the paragraph's supporting ideas in the topic sentence.

The topic sentence should have only a topic and a controlling idea, written in a complete sentence. It should never contain supporting details that belong in the body of the paragraph. Notice that in the following sentences, the support is given in the first sentence. There is nothing left to write in the paragraph.

Examples of "Don't"

1. My mother has a beautiful smile **which makes you feel good when you look at her happy face because she looks cheerful, optimistic, and full of joy.**

2. Going to the beach can be fun **because you can play volleyball, have picnics, or swim.**

3. If you register late for classes at City College, you will have three problems: **the lines will be very long, the classes you want will probably be full, and the best schedules will be taken by other students who have registered early.**

Corrections

1. My mother has a beautiful smile.

2. There are three activities I enjoy when going to the beach with my family.

3. If you try to register late for classes at City College, you will have three problems.

Exercise A2.4   Correct this sentence:

You should not buy a used car from ACE Used Cars because the dealers are often dishonest, there is seldom a guarantee on the car, and the cars are usually overpriced.

_____

_____

Don't #5: Don't forget to focus the topic.

In the following sentences, the topics are too general for one paragraph. The words used as focused topics could mean different things to different readers, so the author's message is not communicated effectively.

Examples of "Don't"

1. **People** have beautiful smiles.

2. **Outdoor activities** can be fun.

3. **Classes** are important.

Corrections

1. My mother has a beautiful smile.

2. There are three activities I enjoy when going to the beach with my family.

3. If you try to register late for classes at City College, you will have three problems.

Exercise A2.5   Look at the corrections for the following topic sentences. Then write a different correctly focused topic sentence for each one.

1. **Education** is important. **(What kind of education? University? Preschool?)**
   Correction

   > **Young children** can benefit from **preschool** education in three important ways.

   Your correction:

   _____

   _____

2. **Crime** is a problem for people. **(What kind of crime? Murder? Shoplifting?)**
   Correction

   > **Student drug dealers at Sunrise High School** are causing **serious** problems **for the school's administrators.**

   Your correction:

   _____

   _____

Don't #6: Don't write more than one focused topic in the topic sentence.

The only type of paragraph that may have two different "topics" is a paragraph of comparison/contrast. In paragraphs of description, you may only have ONE topic per paragraph.

Examples of "Don't"

1. **My mother and my father** have beautiful smiles. **(This topic sentence would require two different paragraphs.)**

2. **Going to the beach or going to the mountains** with your friends can be fun. **(The activities at the beach and those in the mountains are different, so this topic would require two separate sentences.)**

3. **Registering early for classes and applying for financial aid** are complicated procedures. **(Both of these topics would require separate paragraphs.)**

Corrections

1. **My mother** has a beautiful smile.

2. **Going to the beach with friends** can be fun.

3. It is important to **register early for classes** at this college for three reasons.

Exercise A2.6 Correct these topic sentences:

1. **Gabriel García Márquez and Mother Teresa** have both won the Nobel Prize.

   Your correction:

   _____

   _____

2. **Professor Cassidy and Professor Mitchell** have their own unique teaching styles.

   Your correction:

   _____

   _____

Don't #7: Don't omit the topic.

Sometimes, when students write titles for paragraphs, they forget that the focused topic MUST also appear in the topic sentence. A good way to avoid this problem is to write the paragraph first, and then, if your teacher insists on a title for the paragraph, use your focused topic from the topic sentence for your title.

Examples of "Don't"

1. **She** has the most beautiful smile in the world. **(Who is this writer talking about?)**

2. **This** can be fun if you go there with friends. **(What is this writer talking about?)**

3. **It** can cause a serious problem for students registering for classes this semester. **(What is the problem? Financial aid? Long lines?)**

Corrections

1. **My mother** has the most beautiful smile in the world.

2. **Going to the beach** can be fun if you go there with friends.

3. **Not registering early for classes** can cause a serious problem for students at this college.

Exercise A2.7 Correct the following topic sentences. Use a proper noun in place of the pronoun in each sentence.

1. **It** is the worst restaurant in this city.

   Your correction:

   _____

2. **He** is the strangest person I know.

   Your correction:

   _____

Don't #8: Don't omit the controlling idea.

If you omit the controlling idea, your topic sentence may sound like a simple fact that does not need supporting sentences for explanation. The reader won't know what to expect in your paragraph if you do not include a controlling idea.

Examples of "Don't"

1. My mother has blond hair.

2. The beach consists of sand and is located near water.

3. Registration begins on August 10th.

Possible corrections

1. My mother has a beautiful face.

2. Swimming in the ocean can be dangerous.

3. It is important to register early for classes at this college for three reasons.

Exercise A2.8   To correct the following topic sentences, add an interesting controlling idea to each sentence.

1. María has a pet cat.

   Your correction:

   _____

   _____

2. The Earth rotates around the Sun.

   Your correction:

   _____

   _____

Don't #9: Don't write more than one controlling idea.

Each paragraph should develop only ONE controlling idea, so be sure that you do NOT write more than one controlling idea in your topic sentence. In each of the following topic sentences, the controlling idea would require two paragraphs.

Examples of "Don't"

1. My mother has a comical and exotic smile. **(One paragraph could explain "comical," and a separate paragraph could explain "exotic," but these adjectives are not synonyms, so they cannot BOTH be the controlling idea for a single paragraph.)**

2. Going to the beach can be lots of fun, and it can be dangerous or boring. **(This topic sentence contains three different controlling ideas. They are not synonyms. The sentence would require three different paragraphs—not just one.)**

3. Registering early for classes can be easy, and it is important for three reasons. **(At first this topic sentence introduces a process, but then it introduces the idea of "reasons." This topic sentence would require three separate paragraphs.)**

Corrections

1. My mother has an exotic smile.

2. Going to the beach can be dangerous.

3. Registering for classes early is important for three reasons.

Exercise A2.9   Correct the following topic sentences by choosing only one of the controlling ideas in each sentence.

1. Cher is a **talented actress and a popular singer.**

   Your correction:

   _____

2. The 1341 Writing class **is challenging but funny.**

   Your correction:

   _____

Don't #10: Don't use vague words as controlling ideas.

It is important to select the very best and most descriptive adjective you can find for your controlling idea in a paragraph of description. Words such as "good," "bad," "nice," and "interesting" are NOT very descriptive adjectives. They are adjectives that people use when they cannot think of anything more concrete to say. Don't use controlling ideas that do not give the reader a clear picture of what you are going to say about the focused topic.

Examples of "Don't"

1. My mother is **nice. (This controlling idea "nice" does not describe "mother" adequately. There are many more descriptive adjectives that could be used as the controlling idea for one's mother.)**

2. Going to the beach is **interesting.** **(The controlling idea "interesting" is too general. You can use it in your paragraph, but not as the controlling idea in the topic sentence.)**

3. Registering early is a **good thing.** **(There are many more precise controlling ideas than "good." Try to avoid the word "thing" in all academic writing.)**

Alternatives to vague controlling ideas:

Fernando is a **nice** person. **(vague)**

    Fernando has **romantic eyes.**

    Fernando has a **fantastic physique.**

    Fernando is a **gentle person.**

Lorraine is an **interesting** girl. **(vague)**

    Lorraine is **the most intelligent** student in our class.

    Lorraine is **the most eccentric** person I know.

    Lorraine is **crazy.**

Professor Jones is a **bad** teacher. **(vague)**

    Professor Jones's **explanations in class** are **unclear.**

    Professor Jones is **hard to understand.**

    Professor Jones is **unsympathetic to students who are nonnative speakers of English.**

Exercise A2.10 Write your own ORIGINAL corrections for the three examples above.

1. _____

   _____

2. _____

   _____

3. _____

   _____

appendix
three

Irregular Verbs

Base Form	Past Tense	Past Participle
be	was, were	been
become	became	become
begin	began	begun
bend	bent	bent
bite	bit	bitten
blow	blew	blown
break	broke	broken
bring	brought	brought
build	built	built
buy	bought	bought
catch	caught	caught
choose	chose	chosen
come	came	come
cost	cost	cost
cut	cut	cut
do	did	done
draw	drew	drawn
drink	drank	drunk
drive	drove	driven
eat	ate	eaten
fall	fell	fallen
feed	fed	fed
feel	felt	felt

Base Form	Past Tense	Past Participle
fight	fought	fought
find	found	found
fit	fit	fit
fly	flew	flown
forget	forgot	forgotten
forgive	forgave	forgiven
freeze	froze	frozen
get	got	gotten (got)
give	gave	given
go	went	gone
grow	grew	grown
hang	hung	hung
have	had	had
hear	heard	heard
hide	hid	hidden
hit	hit	hit
hold	held	held
hurt	hurt	hurt
keep	kept	kept
know	knew	known
lay	laid	laid
lead	led	led
leave	left	left
let	let	let
lie	lay	lain
light	lit (lighted)	lit (lighted)
lose	lost	lost
make	made	made
mean	meant	meant
meet	met	met
pay	paid	paid
put	put	put

Base Form	Past Tense	Past Participle
quit	quit	quit
read	read	read
ride	rode	ridden
ring	rang	rung
rise	rose	risen
run	ran	run
say	said	said
see	saw	seen
sell	sold	sold
send	sent	sent
set	set	set
shake	shook	shaken
shoot	shot	shot
shut	shut	shut
sing	sang	sung
sit	sat	sat
sleep	slept	slept
slide	slid	slid
speak	spoke	spoken
spend	spent	spent
spread	spread	spread
stand	stood	stood
steal	stole	stolen
stick	stuck	stuck
strike	struck	struck
swear	swore	sworn
sweep	swept	swept
swim	swam	swum
take	took	taken
teach	taught	taught
tear	tore	torn
tell	told	told

Base Form	Past Tense	Past Participle
think	thought	thought
throw	threw	thrown
understand	understood	understood
upset	upset	upset
wake	woke	waked (woken)
wear	wore	worn
win	won	won
withdraw	withdrew	withdrawn
write	wrote	written

appendix four

Spelling and Capitalization Rules

SPELLING RULES

The computer program that accompanies the spelling portion of this section is called "Present and Present Continuous"

1. Adding -s and -es to Nouns and Verbs

   For most nouns, just add -s.

   | the teacher | the teacher**s** | the pen | the pen**s** |
   | the dog | the dog**s** | the chair | the chair**s** |

   When a noun or verb ends in the letters -s, -ss, -sh, -ch, -x, or -z, add -es.

the bus	the bus**es**	the witch	the witch**es**
the kiss	the kiss**es**	the box	the box**es**
the wish	the wish**es**	the waltz	the waltz**es**
I focus it.	She focus**es** it.	I watch it.	She watch**es** it.
I miss you.	She miss**es** you.	I mix them.	She mix**es** them.

   For nouns ending with a consonant and -y, change the -y to -i and add -es.

   | sky | sk**ies** | butterfly | butterfl**ies** |

   For nouns ending with -f or -fe, add -s. Sometimes the -f changes to -v.

   | knife | kni**ves** | loaf | loa**ves** |
   | roof | roo**fs** | cuff | cuf**fs** |

   For nouns that end with -o, add -s or -es.

   | potato | potato**es** | piano | piano**s** |
   | tomato | tomato**es** | buffalo | buffalo**es** |

Some nouns have the same form in the singular and the plural.

moose	**moose**	sheep	**sheep**
French	**French**	fish	**fish**

Some nouns have irregular plural forms.

woman	wom**en**	child	child**ren**
goose	g**ee**se	tooth	t**ee**th

Some nouns have only plural form.

pants   scissors   jeans

Some nouns that look plural are really **singular.**

The United States   news   economics

2. Adding **-ing** to Verbs

When verbs end in -e, drop the -e and add -ing.

bite	bit**ing**	drive	driv**ing**
freeze	freez**ing**	choose	choos**ing**

When verbs end in two consonants, just add -ing.

wish	wish**ing**	sell	sell**ing**
ring	ring**ing**	send	send**ing**

When verbs end in two vowels + one consonant, just add -ing.

meet	meet**ing**	seat	seat**ing**
shot	shoot**ing**	swear	swear**ing**

When verbs end in one vowel + one consonant,[1] AND the word has only one syllable or is stressed on the final syllable, then double the consonant and add -ing.

shut	shú**tt**ing	occúr	occú**rr**ing
plan	plá**nn**ing	forgét	forgé**tt**ing
vísit	vísiting		
óffer	óffering		

When the verb ends in -y, keep the -y and add -ing.

play	pla**ying**	stay	sta**ying**
enjoy	enjo**ying**	buy	bu**ying**

---

1 The exceptions to this rule: never double the final -y or -w. They are not true consonants and are exceptions to most spelling rules. Examples: allow → allowing; play → playing.

When the verb ends in *-ie*, change the *-ie* to *-y* and add *-ing*.

die	d**ying**	lie	l**ying**
tie	t**ying**		

3. Adding *-ed* to Verbs

When regular verbs end in *-e*, add *-d*.

hope	hope**d**	smile	smile**d**
cope	cope**d**	like	like**d**

When regular verbs end in two consonants, just add *-ed*.

wish	wish**ed**	harm	harm**ed**
alarm	alarm**ed**	miss	miss**ed**

When regular verbs end in two vowels + one consonant, just add *-ed*.

wait	wait**ed**	rain	rain**ed**
explain	explain**ed**	maintain	maintain**ed**

When a verb ends in one vowel + one consonant (except *-y* or *-w*), AND the word has only one syllable or is stressed on the final syllable, then double the consonant and add *-ed*.

stop	sto**pp**ed	occúr	occú**rr**ed
plan	pla**nn**ed	admít	admi**tt**ed
visit	vísited		
offer	óffered		

When the verb ends in *-y*, keep the *-y* and add *-ed*.

play	play**ed**	stay	stay**ed**
enjoy	enjoy**ed**	pray	pray**ed**

When the verb ends in *-ie*, just add *-d*.

die	die**d**	lie	lie**d**
tie	tie**d**		

CAPITALIZATION RULES

1. Capitalize the first word of every sentence.

   He came early.

   The teacher was happy.

2. Capitalize the first word of a quotation.

   She asked, "**W**hat are you going to do now?"

   He said, "**T**his is the correct answer."

3. Capitalize family words if they are used as part of a name.

   I sent **A**unt Dorothy a present for her birthday.

   Tell **D**ad that we will be late.

   But do not capitalize family words if they are not used as part of a name.

   My **m**other loves me very much.

   This is my **a**unt, and her name is Marjorie.

4. Capitalize the names of people, including initials and titles.

   James and **M**ark study at this college, but **S**usan studies in Michigan.

   Mr. and **M**rs. **J.** **J**ones are in that office now.

5. Always capitalize the pronoun "I."

   Mary and **I** are going to the beach later.

   He is nicer than **I** am.

6. Capitalize the name of God.

   God   **J**ehovah   **A**llah

7. Capitalize the names of the days of the week, months of the year, and holidays.

   It was **M**onday, **J**une 2, 1874.

   My favorite holiday is the **F**ourth of **J**uly.

   But do not capitalize the names of the seasons.

   spring   **s**ummer   **w**inter   **f**all/**a**utumn

8. Capitalize names of languages, nationalities, races, religions, and peoples.

   English   **E**uropean   **H**ispanic   **C**atholic   **N**ative **A**merican

9. Capitalize the names of countries, states, provinces, counties, and cities.

    Venezuela   **C**alifornia   **M**anitoba   **H**umboldt **C**ounty   **P**ortland

10. Capitalize the names of oceans, lakes, rivers, islands, and mountains.

    the **P**acific **O**cean   **L**ake **O**ntario   **P**eace **R**iver
    Marco **I**sland   the **R**ocky **M**ountains

11. Capitalize geographic areas.

    the **N**ortheast   the **W**est **C**oast   the **M**iddle **E**ast   the **F**ar **E**ast

    But do not capitalize directions if they are not used as part of a geographic area.

    the **n**ortheast section of town   the **s**outhern tip of Chile

12. Capitalize the first word and all words (except prepositions, coordinating conjunctions, and articles) in titles.

    *The **S**ound of **M**usic*   *The **C**hicago **T**ribune*   ***O**ne **S**tep at a **T**ime*

14. Capitalize the names of courses.

    I am studying **W**riting 1241 this semester.

    She says that **C**hemistry 103 is very difficult.

    But do not capitalize these words if they are not the specific name of a course.

    I love to study **c**hemistry. That is why I enrolled for **C**hemistry 103.

    I need to take a **w**riting class. I will register for **W**riting 1341 next term.

Punctuation Rules

END PUNCTUATION

1. Use a period to end a statement or a command.

   The sun is shining today**.**   Go go bed**.**

2. Use a question mark to end a question.

   Where are you going**?**   You are not happy, are you**?**

3. Use an exclamation point to end a sentence that expresses strong emotion.

   Stop**!**   You are going the wrong direction**!**   Good grief**!**

COMMAS

1. Use a comma before a coordinator that connects two complete sentences.

   She studies a lot, yet she fails her tests.

   We went inside, but they stayed outside in the rain.

   But don't use a comma if the sentences are not complete.

   The teacher came in and sat down at the desk.

   We usually travel to California or to Oregon in the summer.

2. Use a comma between items in a series.

   She loves to play tennis, go bowling, and ride horses.

3. Use a comma after the dependent clause if the dependent clause is first in the sentence.[1]

> Because you came early, we will have time to do two of the lessons.

But don't use a comma if the dependent clause comes after the independent clause.

> We will have time to do two of the lessons because you came early.

4. Use a comma after transitional words and expressions (and use a period or semicolon in front of them).

> I hear the phone ringing; however, I am too busy to answer it.
>
> You need to see a dentist. Nevertheless, you refuse to make the appointment.

5. Use a comma in front of expressions like "especially," "such as," "namely," and "for example."

> This college has students from all over the world, especially from South America.
>
> There are many sports one can practice in the winter in Canada, such as skiing and ice skating.

But you can use a colon to introduce a list or an explanation.

> There are three French students in our class: Janine, Pierre, and Etienne.
>
> This class has one outstanding feature: the modern technology used by the teacher.

6. Use a comma after a long introductory clause or phrase.

> After dinner last Sunday evening, we took a walk in the park.
>
> In the evenings, we like to watch the sun setting over the ocean.

7. Use a comma to separate an appositive from the rest of the sentence.

> Professor James, her English teacher, gave her this book to read.
>
> My best friend, Mary Smith, lives in Tampa.

8. Use a comma to separate nonrestrictive relative clauses from the rest of the sentence. A relative clause is nonrestrictive if the information in the clause is not needed to identify the subject of the sentence.

> Jarvis, who was elected chairperson, is from New York.
> (THE INFORMATION IN THE RELATIVE CLAUSE IS NOT NEEDED TO EXPLAIN "WHICH JARVIS.")
>
> The man who was elected chairperson is from New York.
> (THE INFORMATION IN THE RELATIVE CLAUSE IS NEEDED TO EXPLAIN "WHICH MAN.")

---

1 The exceptions to this rule are the subordinators that show a contrast or surprise: *though, although, whereas, while.*

9. Use commas with direct address.

> Mother, can you please come here for a second?
>
> John, please sit down and be still.

10. Use a comma after "yes" and "no" in answers.

> Yes, I will go with you.
>
> No, I will be busy at that time.

11. Use a comma in direct quotations.

> John asked, "Will the test be on Friday?"
>
> The teacher responded, "No, it will be next Wednesday, John."

12. Use a comma with dates, addresses, page references, measurements, and similar information.

> She was born on January 15, 1954, in a small town in California.
>
> Luis moved, and his new address is 12234 Kendall Drive, Miami, Florida.
>
> Julie is five feet, two inches tall.
>
> Page three, section two needs to be revised.

13. Use a comma with coordinate adjectives. Coordinate adjectives are adjectives whose location in the sentence can be changed without changing the meaning of the sentence.

> She has a strange, exotic smile.
>
> This is a dreary, spooky road.

14. Use a comma between contrasting expressions.

> You must study, not play.
>
> This is the end, not the beginning.

SEMICOLONS

Use a semicolon between two complete sentences that are closely related in meaning.

> Some teachers give objective test items; others prefer essay questions.
>
> Miami has a wonderful climate; many tourists go there in the winter.

APOSTROPHES

1. Use apostrophes for contractions.

> We'd better go. **(We HAD better go.)**
>
> We'd rather not do this now. **(We WOULD rather not do this now.)**

2. Use apostrophes to show possession in nouns.

> **singular:** Mary's mother.
>
> > The boy's book. (The book belongs to one boy.)
>
> **plural:** The boys' bathroom. (The bathroom belongs to more than one boy.)
>
> > The men's bathroom. (The bathroom belongs to more than one man.)